Published by Zodiac Publishing UK

Email: general@zodiacpublishing.org
Website: www.zodiacpublishing.org

First published December 2005

ISBN 1-904566-70-7

Printed at International Printing Press, Dubai

ON-ROAD IN

THE UAE

Gareth Leggett

Contents

FEEDER ROUTES

USEFUL INFORMATION

INTRODUCTION

The UAE has some wonderful sights and places to visit by car. It is a rapidly developing society with changes seemingly happening daily. However, with this modern development, people often overlook the natural wonders, not to mention some of the rich history from days gone by. The stark landscapes and at times extreme climate provide a stunning contrast to the vivid green of oases and running water, although with the increased pressure of urban and rural development, flowing water has become a rare sight, particularly in summer. People often make the mistake of thinking that to access these spots you need a 4-wheel drive and a number of very good off road books have been written for the adventurous 4x4 driver and camper. However, the UAE has very good roads and most places can be reached on tarmac, a few extra ones can be reached by travelling on dirt roads, which are easily negotiated by car when dry. This book has been written for all those people who do not have a 4x4 and those with a 4-wheel drive but don't want to go off road. Lately, there has been a trend towards using GPS coordinates, which can be very useful in places where there are no roads. However, most people don't have a GPS, so all the routes in this book, except for a few short diversions, are on marked roads. Thus, it is not necessary to include GPS coordinates and we rely on landmarks and clear simple directions. Each route in this book has written step-by-step directions on the left page and on the

THE UNITED ARAB EMIRATES	
Area:	83,600 sq km
Population:	3.75 million
Capital:	Abu Dhabi
Head of State:	President H.H. Sheikh Khalifa bin Zayed Sultan Al-Nahyan
Official Language:	Arabic
Currency:	UAE dirham (Dh)
Climate:	Temperatures range from a low of 10°C/75.2°F in January, rising to 48°C/105.8°F in July.
Clothing:	Light cottons in summer (July to September), lightweight jackets or pullovers in winter. Sunglasses are advised.

The UAE comprises of 7 emirates: Abu Dhabi. Dubai, Sharjah, Ras Al Khaimah, Fujairah, Ajman and Umm Al Qaiwain.

right, an easy to read line map, eliminating the need to flick through pages in a car to navigate. Each route has a route rating to provide a quick reference of what to expect. Additional feeder routes have been provided for people coming from Dubai or Abu Dhabi to the start of most routes. It aims to provide good directions to interesting places to visit and inform people of some spots they were unaware of and help them to expand their experience of this fascinating country. All the trips can be completed in a day, although, depending on your starting point, you may like to stay overnight at your destination. I have found that, with the excellent road network in the UAE, it is possible to visit any place in the UAE from any other place in the UAE in a day. Though I enjoy driving long distances, it may be better to take a rest and see what is around you rather than watching it flash by the car window. Some may prefer to spend more time exploring in greater detail and the UAE has many good hotels where you can extend your trip. Most of the routes are in the UAE, however, the UAE has a shared border with Oman and you can enter some places from the UAE without the need to cross any border posts. I have taken advantage of this and included a number of routes into Oman. The UAE is much more than shiny modern cities and you don't need a 4x4 to discover its secrets.

PLANNING

The infrastructure in the UAE is very good so only minimal planning is required, but here are some suggestions to help ensure your trip is safe and pleasant:

● Make sure your vehicle is in good working order and services are up to date. Pay particular attention to tyres. The high temperatures encountered in the UAE can place extra stress on them.

● The UAE has a hot and dry climate you should always carry a good supply of drinking water in the car as you can dehydrate very quickly even in winter.

● You should also carry some form of snack in the car. Dates are a good option, but salty biscuits are good too.

● You should carry a basic first aid kit in the car.

● It is also good to have a mobile phone with you.

● The distances between petrol stations in the UAE are usually not that far. However, you should always start a trip with a full tank of fuel. During the trip your fuel consumption should be monitored to ensure you are never in a position where you might run out. It is good to note the petrol stations in Oman on these trips also accept dirhams.

● Toilets in the UAE do not have the best reputation. It is advisable to always carry a roll of toilet paper. If you have not been able to find a toilet and decide to use the countryside, avoid watercourses even if dry, as you never know when it may rain.

● Remember to take extra care if it rains since rain is a very rare occurrence, the roads can become very slippery. It is also not advisable to take a car on dirt roads after heavy rain or to cross flowing wadis.

● It is surprising how cold it can get in winter up in the hills and in the desert at night. Be prepared.

● Make sure you have a hat, sunscreen and sunglasses to protect yourself from the sun.

● Most food stores are open every day, although some shops close early afternoon and reopen in early evening. Many shops do not open on Fridays till the early evening.

● A number of the routes in this book cross into Oman in the shared border area. However, at the time of writing, you do not cross a border post and do not need your passport. Most UAE car insurance covers you in these shared border areas. Please check your insurance before entering Oman.

ROUTE RATING

Each route has a route rating which is broken down into five categories each with a scale ranging from 0-5. The first is **ROAD QUALITY**, which ranges from a 1 (used for Hatta Pools and indicates the need to travel on a rutted road with steep declines and inclines) to a 5, which means that the route is completely on tarmac on good roads. All of the routes, however, are possible with a sedan car. The second category **SHADE/AMENITIES** refers to the amount of shade and amenities along the route and at the destination. The route to Bida bin Saud, for example, has been rated 0 in this category, as there are no shops, toilets or shade at the destination. The third category **ACCESSIBILITY** refers to the ease with which the sites at the destination are readily accessed. The route to Wadi Wurayyah Waterfall, for example, has a rating of 1 since to get down to the waterfall requires a treacherous climb down the side of the wadi, while the route to the top of Jebel Hafeet is a 5 as all the viewing spots are paved car parks. The fourth category **TIME TAKEN** refers to the length of time taken to cover the route and how much time might be taken at the destination or along the route. The route to Liwa has been given a 5 as it is the longest route. However, one should also take into account the time taken to get to the starting point of the route. Finally the fifth category **MY RATING** is my overall feeling about the route and how worthwhile it is to do. As everyone has different interests, you may not always agree with my rating.

ONCE YOU HAVE DECIDED WHERE TO GO

Work out how long it will take you, based on the calculated distance. Make sure you allow time for stopping because the UAE is filled with unexpected sights. Plan carefully what you intend to do at your destination, common activities include: looking at beauty spots, hiking, taking photos, swimming, etc. You may need to bring walking shoes, camera, hat, sunscreen, swimming costume, towel, maybe a picnic. It is no fun arriving and discovering you don't have everything you need to get the most out of the experience.

DRIVING

People tend to drive very fast in the UAE, particularly on the motorways. The speed limit, however, is 120km and the roads do have cameras to catch speeders. Indicating is not widely practiced, nor is lane discipline. These two points mean negotiating roundabouts can be particularly hazardous. Watch out for camels and goats that are roaming free. Sand can blow onto the roads, be careful if this happens as it is not a good idea to hit any piled up sand at speed. The high temperatures cause a haze and a mirage effect on the road and this makes it hard to see oncoming traffic and what is in the distance ahead. It is better to take a bit more time and care getting to your destination than not to arrive at all!

If you are unfortunate enough to have an accident, the cars should not be moved until the police have arrived. Some points to note:

● In event of a serious accident, call the police immediately. Do not move the vehicle.
● Do not leave the scene of the accident.
● For minor accidents, call the police but move the vehicle to the side of the road to avoid blocking the road.

● All accidents must be reported to the police within 24 hours.
● Do not admit liability.
● Do not give money to anyone.
● Do not drive the car unless you are sure it is safe to do so.

PHONE NUMBERS IN CASE OF ACCIDENTS

Police & Emergency	999
Ambulance Services	998
Fire Rescue	997
Operator + Enquiries	181

It is also worth noting that the UAE is in a constant state of development with new roads being built and old ones being redeveloped. At the time of writing, the routes are correct. However, due to this constant change, there may be diversions or road works. The names of places in the book have been taken from what has been displayed on the road signs. You might notice that the names have been spelt differently on different maps and in different publications due to differences in transcription of Arabic to English, but I decided the most helpful spelling would be the one used on the major road signs.

FOLLOWING THE ROUTES

The 17 routes and 5 feeder routes are designed to get you to the destination via the quickest and best road possible. This, however, does not mean that the user should not stop and explore interesting places along the way. Each route has step-by-step directions to get there and on the opposite page a line map of the route where each step refers to the same numbered point on the map. **The line map reads from bottom (starting point) to top (finishing point).** This has been designed to allow one to use the map in the car with the map in the direction the car is moving. The left hand side shows the kilometres you should have covered from the start of the route. Allow for a variance of +/-0.2km to account for different cars and road position.

Next to the kilometres is an arrow indicating the direction in which you should proceed at that point. Next to the arrow is a brief description of the point encountered. Next to this is a symbol depicting the road layout at that point. Refer to the route key page 152 for possibilities. The line map also indicates any points along the route that may be of particular interest, but are not actually part of the route. Petrol stations are also indicated. The route should be easily followed by using the line map, however, the step-by-step instructions provide additional details, should you encounter difficulties. Each route also has a table of kilometres giving you the distance between each step so you can start the route at a different point using the route kilometres table. As well as the routes, a number of feeder routes have been added to provide directions to the start of most routes from Abu Dhabi and Dubai.

Also, at the end of the book, is a satellite road map of the UAE depicting all the major roads. As you can see from this map, the UAE is criss-crossed with a good network of roads, making it easy to get around and explore this interesting part of the world.

Arabic / Muslim Culture

The UAE is an Arabic country and the national religion is Islam. Although the UAE is a very liberal country compared with other Gulf countries, it still has conservative Muslim aspects, which visitors should respect. Women should note that what is acceptable on a Dubai beach is not acceptable off the beach. It is best to dress without revealing too much skin. Men should note that dressing casually in shorts is looked down on although it is becoming commonplace amongst the western ex-patriate community.

Outside the cities, dress more conservatively. Women should cover their upper arms and should wear longer skirts or trousers. It is probably best for women not to travel unaccompanied by a male in country areas to avoid any unwanted attention. Ask before taking a photograph of people, especially of women. During the holy month of Ramadan don't eat, smoke or drink in public. Never drink and drive as it is very unsafe and the penalties are severe.

If visiting the home of a UAE citizen, it is customary to remove shoes before venturing on the carpets and to avoid showing the soles of your feet when sitting down. Non-Muslims are not permitted to enter the mosques.

It is best to dress and act a bit more conservatively than you normally would at home.

NATURE

The UAE is a beautiful country with stunning natural and man-made wonders; however this natural beauty is easily spoiled. Be careful where you drive. Be alert while driving and look out for wildlife crossing the road. Try not to drive over any plants or animals when you pull off the road it is amazing what will emerge after a little bit of rain, once squashed by a vehicle or collected as a souvenir it is unlikely that it will ever spring to life again! The animals of the desert struggle to survive with the finely balanced resources provided in the desert. Be careful not to destroy the few sources of shade or sustenance for them. Once you get out of your vehicle, you will find a harsh and delicately balanced world. It deserves your respect. Please do not spoil it with your litter. Other people want to enjoy it too.

LITTER

Please take home as much litter as you can! If there are no bins or the bins are overflowing take all of your rubbish home to dispose of correctly. Litter is not only unsightly but can also be a hazard for the wild life.

BE A CONSIDERATE PERSON AND DRIVER

Obey the road rules, don't speed or be an aggressive driver. Drive carefully past a person walking or running. Pedestrians have right of way when crossing at a pedestrian crossing. Watch out for cyclists even if thcy are not following the correct road rules. On country roads smile, wave or say hello to people you pass.You never know if you might need their help. Don't play loud music it may be great for you but, others may just want to appreciate the peace and quiet. You have come to see the sights; do not spoil those sights for others.

16

AL AIN TO THE TOP OF JEBEL HAFEET

ROAD QUALITY	✔✔✔✔✔
SHADE/AMENITIES	✔✔✔
ACCESSIBILITY	✔✔✔✔✔
TIME TAKEN	✔
MY RATING	✔✔✔

STARTING POINT:	Al Ain, Sheikha Salama Mosque R/A in the town centre
FINISHING POINT:	Summit of Jebel Hafeet
DISTANCE:	27.4km
ROAD CONDITIONS:	Very good tarred road all the way.
THINGS TO SEE:	Viewing spots, hot springs, Egyptian vultures.
NOTES:	It can be quite cool on the top in winter with the wind chill factor.

Jebel Hafeet, at 1,340 metres, is the highest mountain in the UAE. It is a twisty but fun drive to the top. At the start of the climb up the hill is a hot spring, which has been developed into a park called Green Mubazzerah with places to dip your feet in the hot water and even take a swim. The area around the springs has been heavily planted turning the hills green and contrasting sharply with the stark mountain. They even have a couple of man-made waterfalls. It's a great place to stop for a picnic on the grass under a palm tree.

Near the top of the Jebel Hafeet is the Mecure Grand Hotel with a selection of restaurants with views over Al Ain. There is a coffee shop at the top of Jebel Hafeet where you can buy refreshment.

It is also possible to see Egyptian vultures in the skies above the mountain and goats can be seen scaling the near vertical slopes in their search for food. Fossils can be found in the rocks. The drive up Jebel Hafeet can be taken at anytime of the day or night to get a great view of Al Ain and the surrounding countryside though the view can get a bit hazy in the middle of the day.

DIRECTIONS TO JEBEL HAFEET

1. Zero your odometer at the Sheikha Salama Mosque Roundabout. Drive towards the post office on Zayed Ibn Sultan Street in the opposite direction from the flyover.
2. At the next set of traffic lights turn left. The post office is on the corner on your right.
3. Drive straight down Al Ain Street through a set of traffic lights. The Al Ain Palace Museum is on your left it is a interesting place to look around.
4. Go through another set of traffic lights.
5. Go across a bridge.
6. The Etisalat building is on your left. Turn right at the feed road at the next set of traffic lights onto Khaled Ibn Sultan Street. The feed road should be signposted "Abu Dhabi and Jebel Hafeet".
7. Drive to the next roundabout and turn left onto Khalifa Ibn Zayed Al Awwal Street.
8. Drive straight through a set of traffic lights.
9. Drive straight through another set of traffic lights.
10. Go straight through the roundabout.
11. At the second roundabout with the cement factory on your right, turn left.
12. Drive down the express way to the first off ramp.
13. At the top of the off ramp turn right at the roundabout.
14. Go straight through the next roundabout. Turning right will take you to the Green Mubazzarah (hot springs).
15. At the next roundabout turn left.
16. This feed road will quickly merge with the twisty road to the summit. The road up to the summit has parking view spots at 18.8km, 21.5km, 22.9 km, 23.5 km, 23.7 km, 25.2 km and 26.7km they are all worth a stop.
17. You reach the summit of Jebel Hafeet at 27.4km. It is an enormous open-air car park with a cafeteria, affording nearly 360 degree views.

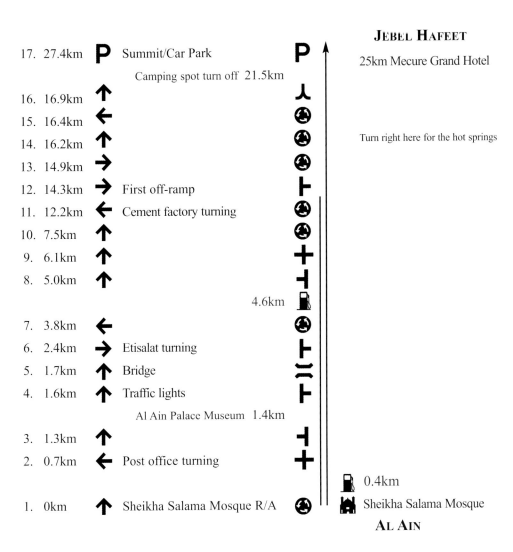

JEBEL HAFEET

17. 27.4km   **P**   Summit/Car Park

25km Mecure Grand Hotel

Camping spot turn off   21.5km

16. 16.9km

15. 16.4km

14. 16.2km

Turn right here for the hot springs

13. 14.9km

12. 14.3km   First off-ramp

11. 12.2km   Cement factory turning

10. 7.5km

9. 6.1km

8. 5.0km

4.6km

7. 3.8km

6. 2.4km   Etisalat turning

5. 1.7km   Bridge

4. 1.6km   Traffic lights

Al Ain Palace Museum   1.4km

3. 1.3km

2. 0.7km   Post office turning

0.4km

1. 0km   Sheikha Salama Mosque R/A   Sheikha Salama Mosque

AL AIN

ROUTE KILOMETRES

Step	Action	km	Distance km	Step	Action	km	Distance km
8.	Go straight	5.0		17.	End	27.4	
			1.2				10.5
7.	Turn left	3.8		16.	Go straight	16.9	
			1.4				0.5
6.	Turn right	2.4		15.	Turn left	16.4	
			0.7				0.2
5.	Go straight	1.7		14.	Go straight	16.2	
			0.1				1.3
4.	Go straight	1.6		13.	Turn right	14.9	
			0.3				0.6
3.	Go straight	1.3		12.	Turn right	14.3	
			0.4				2.1
2.	Turn left	0.7		11.	Turn left	12.2	
			0.7				4.7
1.	Start	0		10.	Go straight	7.5	
							1.4
				9.	Go straight	6.1	
							1.1

OTHER THINGS TO DO IN AL AIN

The oasis city of Al Ain provides an interesting change from the hustle and bustle of Dubai or Abu Dhabi. It is a very green city with trees planted along most roads. You can visit:

● The childhood home of His Highness Sheikh Zayed bin Sultan Al Nahyan, built in 1937, has been restored and is now a museum.
● Hili Archaeological Gardens contains stone-age structures believed to be more than 4000 years old.
● The Al Ain Museum is in the grounds of the Eastern Fort.
● Al Ain has a number of forts and watchtowers.

● The oases of Al Ain and Qattarah provide pleasant spots to stroll around. It is much cooler in an oasis.
● Numerous parks and gardens and landscaped roundabouts.
● The camel market.
● The zoo and aquarium noted for its large herd of Arabian oryx.

AL AIN TO KHADRA

ROAD QUALITY	✔✔✔✔
SHADE/AMENITIES	✔
ACCESSIBILITY	✔✔✔✔
TIME TAKEN	✔✔
MY RATING	✔✔✔

STARTING POINT:	Al Ain, Sheikha Salama Mosque R/A in the town centre
FINISHING POINT:	Khadra
DISTANCE:	49.5km
ROAD CONDITIONS:	Very good tarred road all the way.
THINGS TO SEE:	Gravel plains, flowing water, goats, side-trip to Fossil Valley
NOTES:	Water can dry up in summer months.

Khadra is a wonderful spot, just a short drive from Al Ain into Oman and you do not have to cross a border post to get there. The wadi at Khadra is usually flowing with water, not much, but it is flowing. It can, however, dry up during the summer. It is amazing to see water flowing in the gravel plains, which are almost moon-like. The first wadi crossing at Khadra has been set up as a bit of a picnic spot with shade pagodas.

Walking down the wadi you come across interesting rock formations, the further you are willing to hike, the more interesting they become. Khadra also has a date palm oasis and pools that you can swim in. At the end of the pools, you can wade through the water into a narrow gorge following the water to its source. Additionally, just before you get to the pools, are some interesting ruins, extensive stonewalls and aflaj harking back to a time when the wadi flowed stronger. It's a great spot for a picnic especially in winter. For the more adventurous, it is also a good spot to camp since the areas enclosed by the stone walls are cleared of stones and provide a flat smooth surface to camp on in a very rocky area.

The route to Khadra passes Fossil Valley, which can provide an entertaining stop as well as a chance to take in the panoramic views page 29.

A side trip to Mahdah can also be taken where there is an old restored fort.

DIRECTIONS TO KHADRA

1. Zero your odometer at the Sheikha Salama Mosque R/A. Drive down Salahuddeen Al Ayyubi Street with the mosque on your right hand side.
2. At next roundabout, with Pizza Hut on the opposite corner, turn right.
3. Drive straight down Khalifa Ibn Zayed Street to the next set of traffic lights and turn left onto Abu Baker Al Siddiq Street.
4. Turn right at the next roundabout signposted Mezyad.
5. Drive down Shakhboot Ibn Sultan Street to the next roundabout and go all the way round it until you are returning in the direction you just came from.
6. At the next set of traffic lights take the feed road to the right signposted to Buraimi. Cross the Omani border at the 'Peace be with you' sign.
7. Go straight across the bridge at 5.5km and then another at 5.9km.
8. At the next roundabout, Hesn R/A, take the feed road to the right signposted Muscat / Salalah.
9. Go straight to the next roundabout Sharia'a R/A and turn left, signposted to Al Khadra.
10. As you approach the next roundabout, Mosque R/A, you will see a big mosque on the opposite side. Take the second road on your right signposted Al Jizi / Sohar. Drive past the Burami Hotel on your left
11. Turn left at the next roundabout Hospital R/A. The road is signposted to Mahdah. After about 2.5 kms you will come across the Buraimi Industrial Estate on your left. Continue straight on.
12. Further along this road, you will pass the sign to the sewerage works. This is the road to access Fossil Valley on your right page 29.
13. Continue straight and turn left on the road for the Wadi Al Qahfi Camp Site this turning is also signposted to Mahdah H.C. and Al Rodha.
14. Drive to the next roundabout and go straight through it to the road signposted to Al Juwaif.
15. After crossing 3 smaller wadi crossings at about 4.5 km after the roundabout the road will dip down to cross a wadi.
16. 5.6km from the roundabout is the turning for Khadra on the right. Drive down the Khadra road, you should reach the wadi crossing after 7.5km.
17. At the wadi crossing, the road becomes dirt but a saloon car can easily drive into Khadra. On the other side of Khadra, there is another wadi crossing and the start of Khadra Oasis.

17. 49.5km **P** Wadi crossing   ▪▪▪▪ ↑ **KHADRA**
              To Khadra Pools   49km

16. 42.0km →   ⊢
15. 40.9km ↑ Wadi crossing   ▪▪▪▪
14. 36.4km ↑
13. 33.0km ←   ⊤⊢
12. 21.5km ↑ Turning for Fossil Valley   ⊢   ◉ Fossil Valley
11. 10.3km ← Hospital R/A   ◎
              Buraimi Hotel 9.7km   🅿 8.7km

10. 8.3km → 2nd right Mosque R/A   ◎
9. 7.1km ← Sharia'a R/A   ◎
8. 6.1km → Hesn R/A   🏰   ◎
7. 5.9km   6km   Oman border 4.7km
    5.5km ↑   4.8km 🅿   ≡
6. 4.3km → Turning for Buraimi   ⊢
5. 2.7km ∩   ◎
4. 1.2km →   ◎

3. 0.8km ←   ✚
2. 0.3km →   ◎

1. 0km   ↑ Sheikha Salama Mosque R/A   ◎   🕌 Sheikha Salama Mosque
                                               AL AIN

ROUTE KILOMETRES

Step	Action	km	Distance km	Step	Action	km	Distance km
8.	Turn right	6.1		17.	End	49.5	
			0.6				7.5
7.	Go straight	5.5		16.	Turn right	42	
			1.2				1.1
6.	Turn right	4.3		15.	Go straight	40.9	
			1.6				4.5
5.	U turn	2.7		14.	Go straight	36.4	
			1.5				3.4
4.	Turn right	1.2		13.	Turn left	33	
			0.4				11.5
3.	Turn left	0.8		12.	Go straight	21.5	
			0.5				11.2
2.	Turn right	0.3		11.	Turn left	10.3	
			0.3				2.0
1.	Start	0		10.	2nd right	8.3	
							1.2
				9.	Turn left	7.1	
							1.0

SIDE TRIP - FOSSIL VALLEY

On the road out of Buraimi you pass by Fossil Valley. There are more than just fossils here. 11.2km along the Mahdah road from the roundabout after the Buraimi Hotel, you will come across a sign to the right for the sewage treatment works. This is the turning for Fossil Valley. About 200 metres down the road, on your right hand side, there is a ridge of rocks which is reputed to be an ancient reef that has been pushed up over millions of years to reveal itself. You can stop anywhere along this road and explore the ridge for fossils. The top of the ridge provides a good spot to catch the setting sun over Buraimi. Also turn around to get a great view of the impressive rock faces of Jebel Qatar. On the other side of the ridge, there are a few trees that could provide some shade for a picnic.

The sewage treatment plant at the end of the road also provides an oasis for bird life and its rich green vegetation, not only provides a haven for the birds, but also provides a stark contrast against the surrounding dry desert mountains.

SIDE TRIPS - KHADRA POOLS

As a side trip, you can reach Khadra Pools by going down a dirt road which is about 0.5km before the wadi crossing on your right as you approach it coming from the wadi. This dirt road does become a bit rocky and not everyone will feel comfortable negotiating it by saloon car. Drive past the houses on your right and turn right on the track after the track to the houses. This track will bypass the houses and head to the wadi. You will know you are near the first pool when you see a piece of open ground surrounded on three sides by stone walls, leave your car here. Just before the old stone walls on your left is a dirt football pitch. If you don't mind a few hundred yards extra walk and no one is playing football, you can park here if you feel the road is getting a bit too rough. Clamber down to the wadi. Walk along the wadi and, where it joins another wadi, back to your right is the first pool. The second pool is ahead along the track about 800 metres. You will see power lines crossing the wadi, park here. You will not see either pool from the edge of the wadi. You need to walk down to the wadi floor. However, the pools and associated gorges are worth the trip. It is strange how water appears and disappears and transforms first into a stream or pool and later into a dry wadi.

Another side trip is to cross the wadi and go in Khadra village. Once you have passed through the village there is another wadi crossing. If you cross that you enter the oasis. It may, however, be better to explore the oasis on foot, as the road gets a bit rougher and narrower.

AL AIN TO KHUTWA

ROAD QUALITY	✔✔✔
SHADE/AMENITIES	✔✔✔
ACCESSIBILITY	✔✔
TIME TAKEN	✔✔✔
MY RATING	✔✔✔✔

STARTING POINT:	Al Ain, Sheikha Salama Mosque R/A in the town centre
FINISHING POINT:	Old Khutwa
DISTANCE:	55.1km
ROAD CONDITIONS:	Very good, tarred road all the way, except for the last 2km on dirt, but worth the trip.
THINGS TO SEE:	Oasis nestled in the hills, deep narrow gorges with running water, water pools and a working oasis.
NOTES:	Unlocked cars are likely to be broken into in Khutwa. Lock your car and do not leave valuables in it.

Khutwa is a stunning oasis nestled in the hills. Your first sight of it as you come over the hill makes a great picture with the intense green of the date palms contrasting against the dark rugged mountains.

Once into the oasis is a fascinating vision of what can be cultivated, even in this arid country when the right approach is taken. Khutwa's other stunning features are 2 deep narrow gorges carved into the rock by the water flowing in the wadi. Exploring these gorges is fascinating and provides many photo opportunities. If that is not enough, Khutwa even has pools.

To get to Khutwa you drive through the barren gravel desert at the base of the mountains surrounding Buraimi. This is a great spot to visit to have a picnic and to explore. It can be very popular during holidays.

33

DIRECTIONS TO KHUTWA

1. Zero your odometer at the Sheikha Salama Mosque R/A. Drive down Salahuddeen Al Ayyubi Street with the mosque on your right hand side.
2. At next roundabout, with Pizza Hut on the opposite corner, turn right.
3. Drive straight down Khalifa Ibn Zayed Street to the next set of traffic lights and turn left on to Abu Baker Al Siddiq Street.
4. Turn right at the next roundabout signposted Mezyad.
5. Drive down Shakhboot Ibn Sultan Street to the next roundabout and go all the way round it until you are going in the direction you just came from.
6. At the next set of traffic lights take the feed road to the right heading signposted to Buraimi. You will shortly cross the Oman border at the 'Peace be with you' sign.
7. Go straight across the bridge at 5.5km and then another at 5.9km.
8. At the next roundabout Hesn R/A take the feed road to the right signposted Muscat/Salalah.
9. Go straight to the next roundabout Sharia'a R/A and turn left signposted to Al Khadra.
10. As you approach the next roundabout Mosque R/A a big mosque will be seen on the opposite side. Take the second road on your right signposted Al Jizi / Sohar. Drive past the Buraimi hotel on your left.
11. Go straight through Hospital R/A you are on the Buraimi/Sohar road. After about 18km you will pass through a V-shaped mountain crossing cut out of the mountain.
12. Go straight across the bridge.
13. At the next roundabout, turn left. Turn right here to get to Al Ain crossing the UAE border but as you did not enter Oman this way it is best to leave the way you came in.
14.-18. This road will cross 5 bridges crossing dry wadis.
19. After another 6.2km there is a mosque, turn left here (signposted to Mahdah).
20. This road will cross 1 bridge across a dry wadi
21. After 5km you should reach a turning to the right to Khutwa. Take it and after another 3km you will reach the new village of Khutwa.
22. Proceed through the village the road will turn to gravel just the other side of the village.
23. The road will climb up a hill. Be prepared for the great view as you go over the crest of the hill. It's worth stopping to take it in. Proceed down the hill and you enter the old village of Khutwa.
24. You will come across a clearing on your left, which can be used for parking.
25. However, you can proceed on through the village on a narrow twisty track and into the oasis to a square with a small mosque in the right hand corner park here and proceed on foot to the gorge.

34

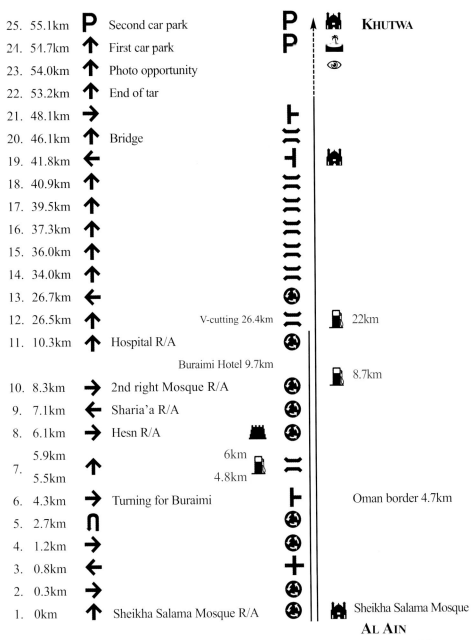

25.	55.1km	**P** Second car park
24.	54.7km	↑ First car park
23.	54.0km	↑ Photo opportunity
22.	53.2km	↑ End of tar
21.	48.1km	→
20.	46.1km	↑ Bridge
19.	41.8km	←
18.	40.9km	↑
17.	39.5km	↑
16.	37.3km	↑
15.	36.0km	↑
14.	34.0km	↑
13.	26.7km	←
12.	26.5km	↑ V-cutting 26.4km
11.	10.3km	↑ Hospital R/A
		Buraimi Hotel 9.7km
10.	8.3km	→ 2nd right Mosque R/A
9.	7.1km	← Sharia'a R/A
8.	6.1km	→ Hesn R/A
7.	5.9km	↑ 6km
	5.5km	4.8km
6.	4.3km	→ Turning for Buraimi
5.	2.7km	∩
4.	1.2km	→
3.	0.8km	←
2.	0.3km	→
1.	0km	↑ Sheikha Salama Mosque R/A

P   **KHUTWA**
P

22km

8.7km

Oman border 4.7km

Sheikha Salama Mosque

AL AIN

35

ROUTE KILOMETRES

STEP	ACTION	KM	DISTANCE KM	STEP	ACTION	KM	DISTANCE KM
13.	Turn left	26.7		25.	End	55.1	
			0.2				0.4
12.	Go straight	26.5		24.	Go straight	54.7	
			16.2				0.7
11.	Go straight	10.3		23.	Go straight	54.0	
			2.0				0.8
10.	2nd right	8.3		22.	Go straight	53.2	
			1.2				5.1
9.	Turn left	7.1		21.	Turn right	48.1	
			1.0				2.0
8.	Turn right	6.1		20.	Go straight	46.1	
			0.6				4.3
7.	Go straight	5.5		19.	Turn left	41.8	
			1.2				0.9
6.	Turn right	4.3		18.	Go straight	40.9	
			1.6				1.4
5.	U turn	2.7		17.	Go straight	39.5	
			1.5				2.2
4.	Turn right	1.2		16.	Go straight	37.3	
			0.4				1.3
3.	Turn left	0.8		15.	Go straight	36.0	
			0.5				2.0
2.	Turn right	0.3		14.	Go straight	34.0	
			0.3				7.3
1.	Start	0					

SIDE TRIP - KHUTWA GORGE AND POOLS

Once you have parked at the mosque, proceed on foot. There is a path to the left of the mosque, follow that. It bears right and you cross a falaj just past the mosque. Continue following the path it will come to a point over-looking the gorge. Proceed down the path, following it across the top of the gorge. A concrete bridge has been constructed across the narrow gorge. It provides for a good spot to look down and along the gorge. Cross the bridge, the path continues on to another concrete bridge crossing the parallel gorge. To get to the pools, before reaching the second bridge, turn left and walk across the top of the gorge and you will soon reach one of the pools.

A QUICK DIP INTO BURAIMI

ROAD QUALITY	✔✔✔
SHADE/AMENITIES	✔✔✔
ACCESSIBILITY	✔✔✔
TIME TAKEN	✔✔✔✔
MY RATING	✔✔✔✔

STARTING POINT:	Al Ain/Oman border
FINISHING POINT:	Oman border
DISTANCE:	107.3km
ROAD CONDITIONS:	Very good tarred road all the way, except for 2km on dirt to Khutwa but worth the trip
THINGS TO SEE:	Fossil valley, oasis nestled in the hills, gorges, water pools and a working oasis, forts, Buraimi Souq
NOTES:	Unlocked cars are likely to be broken into in Khutwa. Lock your car and do not leave valuables in it.

It is possible to get a good feeling of Oman with a quick dip into Buraimi. Here is a suggested route to do if you do not have time to do the Buraimi routes individually. You head along the route to Khadra passing the Buraimi Hotel and head in the direction of Fossil Valley where you can stop to take in the view and see if you can spot any fossils in the rocks. Then, continue on the route to Khadra but do not take the turning for Khadra, continue on to Mahdah, a village with a restored fort, at the far end.

You can stop to explore or continue on along the road till you reach the Khutwa turnoff 14 km from Mahdah. Turn left into this, drive through the new village and onto the dirt road (it is worth it) and up to the top of the rise and stop to take in one of the best views and picture opportunities in the book.

Now continue on to Khutwa to explore the oasis and the gorge. Once you have finished with Khutwa, return to Buraimi along the route for Khutwa through the V-cutting. At the Hesn Roundabout, instead of heading back to Al Ain, go straight and you have the choice of exploring the old and new souqs as well as a couple of restored forts on the edge of the Buraimi Oasis. There is also a quirky little antique store where you can pick up a mixture of fascinating items.

DIRECTIONS FOR A QUICK DIP INTO BURAIMI

1.   This route starts as you cross the Oman border into Buraimi from Al Ain at the green Wilyat Buraimi sign.
2.   Go straight across the bridge at 0.7km and another at 1.1km.
3.   At the next roundabout (Hesn R/A) take the feed road to the right signposted Muscat / Salalah.
4.   Go straight to the next roundabout Sharia'a R/A and turn left signposted to Al Khadra.
5.   As you approach the next roundabout (Mosque R/A) you will see a big mosque on the opposite side. Take the second road on your right signposted Al Jizi / Sohar. Drive past the Buraimi Hotel on your left.
6.   Turn left at the next roundabout. The road is signposted to Mahdah. After about 2.5 kms you will come across the Buraimi Industrial Estate on your left. Continue straight on.
7.   Further along this road, you will pass the sign to the sewerage works. This is the road to access Fossil Valley page 29 on your right. Turn right here.
8.   Drive along the road towards the sewage works pull over onto the side of the road on your right hand side. On and behind this exposed ridge you might see some fossils and will get an excellent view of the valley.
9.   Once you have had enough of Fossil Valley; pull a u-turn to head back the way you came.
10. Turn right at the T-junction heading for Mahdah H.C.
11. Continue straight past the left turn for the Wadi Al Qahfi Camp Site this turning is also signposted to Mahdah H.C. and Al Rodha. You can turn here for Khadra and for Hatta.
12. Continue straight past the turning for Mahdah.
13. The next turn for Aboul has an old restored fort on the corner.
14. Go straight past the turning for Mussah.
15. Go straight past the turning for Al Musaidah.
16. Turn left at the turning for Khutwa. After 3 km you will reach the new village of Khutwa.
17. Proceed through the village the road will turn to gravel just the other side of the village.
18. The road will climb up a hill. Be prepared for the great view as you go over the crest of the hill. It's worth stopping to take it in. Proceed down the hill and you enter the old village of Khutwa.
19. You will come across a clearing on your left, which can be used for parking.
20. However, you can proceed on through the village on a narrow twisty track and into the oasis to a square with a small mosque in the right hand corner park here and proceed on foot to the gorge.

CONTINUED ON PAGE 43

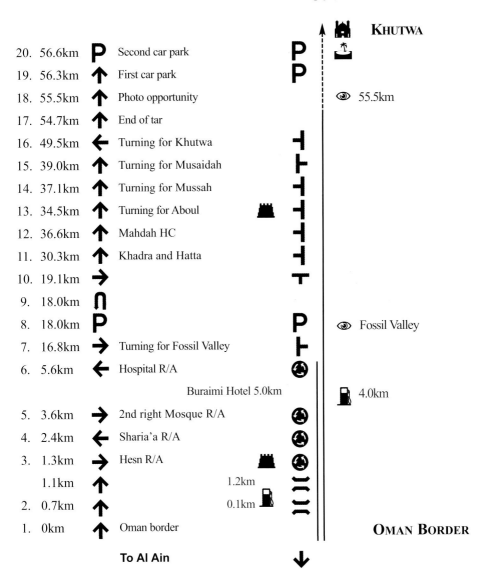

KHUTWA

20. 56.6km P Second car park   P
19. 56.3km ↑ First car park   P
18. 55.5km ↑ Photo opportunity   55.5km
17. 54.7km ↑ End of tar
16. 49.5km ← Turning for Khutwa
15. 39.0km ↑ Turning for Musaidah
14. 37.1km ↑ Turning for Mussah
13. 34.5km ↑ Turning for Aboul
12. 36.6km ↑ Mahdah HC
11. 30.3km ↑ Khadra and Hatta
10. 19.1km →
9. 18.0km ∩
8. 18.0km P   Fossil Valley
7. 16.8km → Turning for Fossil Valley
6. 5.6km   ← Hospital R/A
               Buraimi Hotel 5.0km   4.0km
5. 3.6km   → 2nd right Mosque R/A
4. 2.4km   ← Sharia'a R/A
3. 1.3km   → Hesn R/A
    1.1km   ↑   1.2km
2. 0.7km   ↑   0.1km
1. 0km   ↑ Oman border   OMAN BORDER

            To Al Ain   ↓

41

21.	Refer to page 27 for details on directions to gorge and pools.
22.	Turn around and go back the way you came.
23.	Go past the first carpark
24.	Go over the hill with the good view over old Khutwa.
25.	The tar starts here, drive through new Khutwa.
26.	At the T-junction turn left.
27.	Cross the bridge.
28.	Go straight past the turning for Dahir.
29.	Turn right at the T-junction with the mosque opposite you.
30-34.	Cross five bridges.
35.	Go straight past the turning for Musaidrah.
36.	At the roundabout turn right signposted to Buraimi. Al Ain is signposted straight ahead but that will take you to the UAE border post and as you have not come through that way it is best to go back through Buraimi.
37.	Cross the bridge and go through the V-cutting.
38.	Go straight through the Hospital R/A and pass the Buraimi Hotel on your right.
39.	At the oval roundabout (Mosque R/A) with the mosque on your right turn left.
40.	At the next roundabout turn right.
41.	At the Hesn R/A (near the souq) go straight. The old souq will be on your right there is some parking to your right near the old souq but the car park is usually occupied by stalls.
42.	Turn left at the T-junction and shortly after the turn there is some parking on your right should you wish to stop and explore the souqs.
43.	Cross the bridge.
44.	Continue to the next T-junction on your left will be Fort Antiques an interesting shop to visit and on your right is the impressively restored Al Khandaq Fort. It is worth stopping to have a walk around the fort. At the junction turn left.
45.	At the next T-junction turn right.
46.	Cross the bridge.
47.	You will shortly cross the Oman border back into the UAE.

A Quick Dip into Buraimi

To Al Ain   ↑   **OMAN BORDER**

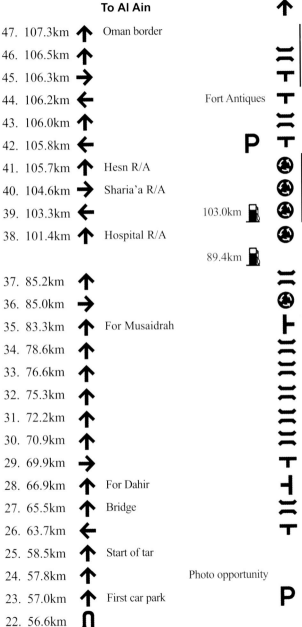

47. 107.3km ↑	Oman border	Police check point
46. 106.5km ↑		107.1km
45. 106.3km →		
44. 106.2km ←	Fort Antiques	Al Khandaq Fort
43. 106.0km ↑		
42. 105.8km ←	P	Fort P
41. 105.7km ↑	Hesn R/A	
40. 104.6km →	Sharia'a R/A	
39. 103.3km ←	103.0km	Buraimi Hotel 102.0km
38. 101.4km ↑	Hospital R/A	
	89.4km	
37. 85.2km ↑		V-cutting 85.3km
36. 85.0km →		
35. 83.3km ↑	For Musaidrah	
34. 78.6km ↑		
33. 76.6km ↑		
32. 75.3km ↑		
31. 72.2km ↑		
30. 70.9km ↑		
29. 69.9km →		
28. 66.9km ↑	For Dahir	
27. 65.5km ↑	Bridge	
26. 63.7km ←		
25. 58.5km ↑	Start of tar	
24. 57.8km ↑	Photo opportunity	
23. 57.0km ↑	First car park	P
22. 56.6km ∩		

CONTINUED FROM PAGE 41

43

ROUTE KILOMETRES

STEP	ACTION	KM	DISTANCE KM
24.	Go straight	57.8	
			0.8
23.	Go straight	57.0	
			0.4
22.	U turn	56.6	
			0
21.	Walk to gorge		
			0
20.	Park	56.6	
			0.3
19.	Go straight	56.3	
			0.8
18.	Go straight	55.5	
			0.8
17.	Go straight	54.7	
			5.2
16.	Turn left	49.5	
			10.5
15.	Go straight	39.0	
			1.9
14.	Go straight	37.1	
			2.6
13.	Go straight	34.5	
			0.9
12.	Go straight	33.6	
			3.3
11.	Go straight	30.3	
			11.2
10.	Turn right	19.1	
			1.1
9.	U turn	18.0	
			0
8.	Park	18.0	
			1.2
7.	Turn right	16.8	
			11.2
6.	Turn left	5.6	
			2.0
5.	2nd right	3.6	
			1.2
4.	Turn left	2.4	
			1.1
3.	Turn right	1.3	
			0.6
2.	Go straight	0.7	
			0.7
1.	Go straight	0	

STEP	ACTION	KM	DISTANCE KM
47.	End	107.3	
			0.8
46.	Go straight	106.5	
			0.2
45.	Turn right	106.3	
			0.1
44.	Turn left	106.2	
			0.2
43.	Go straight	106.0	
			0.2
42.	Turn left	105.8	
			0.1
41.	Go straight	105.7	
			1.1
40.	Turn right	104.6	
			1.3
39.	Turn left	103.3	
			1.9
38.	Go straight	101.4	
			16.2
37.	Go straight	85.2	
			0.2
36.	Turn right	85.0	
			1.7
35.	Go straight	83.3	
			4.7
34.	Go straight	78.6	
			2.0
33.	Go straight	76.6	
			1.3
32.	Go straight	75.3	
			3.1
31.	Go straight	72.2	
			1.3
30.	Go straight	70.9	
			1.0
29.	Turn right	69.9	
			3.0
28.	Go straight	66.9	
			1.4
27.	Go straight	65.5	
			1.8
26.	Turn left	63.7	
			5.2
25.	Go straight	58.5	
			0.7

THE FALAJ AND THE OASIS

For thousands of years, people in the Gulf region have relied on the aflaj (singular falaj) to provide water for agriculture as well as domestic use. Although the modern cities of the UAE now rely on piped water or large water tanks, rural villages still use the aflaj for irrigation of the palm plantations and even personal use. The aflaj use a system of tapping underground water or water from mountain streams which is then led by man-made channels and tunnels to villages. Some aflaj consist of a well and channels underground, but tourists will usually see those that consist of shallow wells tapping water from the wadi (seasonal river) bank with open channels. Remnants of ancient stone channels can be seen at various locations in the UAE, for example, near the Khadra pools and some modern falaj channels are in fact reconstructions or improvements of ancient falaj channels. Modern falaj channels are usually of cement. The aflaj nourish the entire oasis which is planted in layers: the date palms provide a canopy to shield lower trees like banana from the searing heat and these in turn protect low bushes or fields of fodder. The aflaj system is opened and closed at set intervals and water floods the area around a tree or group of trees, but each plant gets just enough to grow and not a precious drop is wasted.

AL AIN TO AL QUA'A

ROAD QUALITY	✔✔✔✔
SHADE/AMENITIES	✔✔
ACCESSIBILITY	✔✔✔✔
TIME TAKEN	✔✔✔
MY RATING	✔✔✔

STARTING POINT:	Al Ain, Sheikha Salama Mosque R/A in the town centre
FINISHING POINT:	Al Qua'a/Oman Border fence
DISTANCE:	124.1km
ROAD CONDITIONS:	Good tarred road
THINGS TO SEE:	Dramatic dunes, Oman border fence, camels, small lake, man-made forests in the desert and numerous farms and date plantations.
NOTES:	Beware of the many, enormous speed-humps as well as cars overtaking trucks on blind-rises and across solid white lines.

The route from Al Ain to Al Qua'a reveals the true Arabia - dramatic dunes contrasted with the green of oasis. This area is not an "empty quarter" at all, but encompasses a diverse, fascinating spectacle of ochre and beige sands and the vivid green of farms, date plantations and even man-made "forests". A small lake provides a haven for bird-life and the route is one of the best for seeing camels and of course the ubiquitous goats. The road hugs the UAE/Oman border dividing the spoils of dramatic dunes in two and culminates at the border between the two countries. The border fence can be glimpsed, periodically on the route snaking its way through the dunes and the odd Omani camel can be seen looking longingly through the fence at the greenery across the border.

The route is well-travelled by trucks laden with fodder for the hungry camels. At the time of writing a lot of construction was going on at the side of the road as they are building a duel carriageway the length of the route.

DIRECTIONS TO AL QUA'A

1. Zero your odometer at the Sheikha Salama Mosque R/A. Drive towards the post office on Zayed Ibn Sultan Street in the opposite direction from the flyover.
2. At the next set of traffic lights turn left. The post office is on the corner on your right as you make the turn.
3. Drive straight down Al Ain Street through a set of traffic lights.
4. Go through another set of traffic lights.
5. Go across a bridge.
6. The Etisalat building should be coming up on your left. Turn right at the feed road at the next set of traffic lights onto Khaled Ibn Sultan Street. The feed road should be signposted Abu Dhabi and Jebel Hafeet.
7. Drive to the next roundabout and turn left onto Khalifa Ibn Zayed Al Awwal Street.
8. Drive straight through a set of traffic lights.
9. Drive straight through another set of traffic lights.
10. Go straight through the next roundabout.
11. Go straight through the next roundabout with the cement factory on your right.
12. Turn left at the next roundabout onto Hazaa Ibn Sultan Street
13. At the next roundabout (Mountain Goat R/A) go straight. You can turn left here for Green Mubuzzarah (hot springs).
14. You will soon come across the Ain Al Fayda sign and turning. You should pass it on your right. Continue straight towards Al Wagan. Shortly after Ain Al Fayda the road will change from duel carriageway to single carriageway.
15. You will follow this road till the end of the journey. Drive past many magnificent dunes, man-made forests, farms and date plantations. You can go right here for Al Wagon.
16. You drive through the edge of Al Qua'a.
17. Drive past the turning for Um El Zunool.
18. The road will bear right signposted to Um El Zumool. This route ends by driving straight (instead of turning right) on towards the Oman border fence, which crosses and ends the road.

AL QUA'A

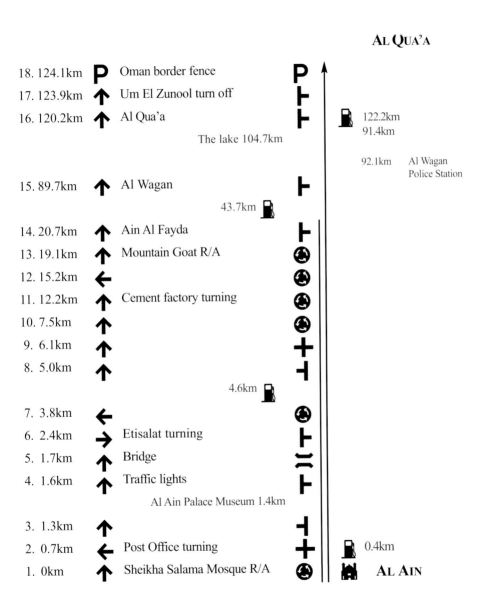

18. 124.1km — Oman border fence

17. 123.9km — Um El Zunool turn off

16. 120.2km — Al Qua'a

            The lake 104.7km

122.2km
91.4km

92.1km   Al Wagan
Police Station

15. 89.7km — Al Wagan

            43.7km

14. 20.7km — Ain Al Fayda

13. 19.1km — Mountain Goat R/A

12. 15.2km

11. 12.2km — Cement factory turning

10. 7.5km

9. 6.1km

8. 5.0km

            4.6km

7. 3.8km

6. 2.4km — Etisalat turning

5. 1.7km — Bridge

4. 1.6km — Traffic lights

            Al Ain Palace Museum 1.4km

3. 1.3km

2. 0.7km — Post Office turning

1. 0km — Sheikha Salama Mosque R/A

0.4km

AL AIN

ROUTE KILOMETRES

STEP	ACTION	KM	DISTANCE KM	STEP	ACTION	KM	DISTANCE KM
9.	Go straight	6.1		18.	End	124.1	
			1.1				0.2
8.	Go straight	5.0		17.	Go straight	123.9	
			1.2				3.7
7.	Turn left	3.8		16.	Go straight	120.2	
			1.4				30.5
6.	Turn right	2.4		15.	Turn left	89.7	
			0.7				69.0
5.	Go straight	1.7		14.	Go straight	20.7	
			0.1				1.6
4.	Go straight	1.6		13.	Turn right	19.1	
			0.3				3.9
3.	Go straight	1.3		12.	Turn right	15.2	
			0.6				3.0
2.	Turn left	0.7		11.	Turn left	12.2	
			0.7				4.6
1.	Start	0		10.	Go straight	7.5	
							1.4

THE LAKE IN THE DESERT

The road to Al Qua'a is a great way to see huge rolling sand dunes and the extensive efforts on the part of the UAE government to tame the land and make it agriculturally productive. For a good part of the route out of Al Ain the road has been lined with irrigated trees. This, in addition to the date palm plantations and the extensive planting of trees, creates forests in the desert, surreal images as the dunes loom menacingly over the strip of green along the road. It is surprising out here to find a small lake bordered with reeds under one of these dunes. You will find the lake at 104.7km along the route on the left hand side of the road. It might be better to stop for a look on the way back, 20 km from the end of the route on your right. You will see a glimpse of reeds at the foot of a large dune. Pull over after the end of a curb and walk back in the direction you came along the edge of the cliff and you will find this haven for birds in the dry desert.

AL AIN TO BIDA BINT SAUD

ROAD QUALITY	✔✔✔✔✔
SHADE/AMENITIES	*See notes*
ACCESSIBILITY	✔✔
TIME TAKEN	✔
MY RATING	✔✔✔✔

STARTING POINT:	Al Ain, Sheikha Salama Mosque R/A in the town centre
FINISHING POINT:	Bida bint Saud
DISTANCE:	20.9km
ROAD CONDITIONS:	Very good tarred road all the way.
THINGS TO SEE:	Bida bint Saud, old tombs, camels and lots of dunes.
NOTES:	There is no shade from the sun so bring whatever protection you need.

The outcrop known as Bida bint Saud lies amongst rolling red dunes just a stone's throw from the oasis town of Al Ain. This route provides a fascinating spectacle for the amateur archaeologist. The route proceeds through the centre of Al Ain, past its numerous ornamental roundabouts in a northerly direction, heading out of Al Ain towards the Dubai road.

On the way, you will pass turnoffs for the oases of Qattara, Al Jimi and Hili as well as for Hili Archaeological Gardens. Hili Archaeological Gardens contains the imposing Hili Tower, a circular stone tomb believed to be more than 4000 years old as well as other tombs and evidence of Iron Age settlements, while other prominent tombs can be seen at Qattara Oasis. Hili Oasis boasts the restored Hili Fort and the Muraijib Fort, built in 1816 is near Qattara Oasis. After 10 kms through Al Ain on dual-carriageway roads, the route continues on a narrow road with numerous speed bumps between red dunes. You will soon sight your first camel and be amazed to see a walled compound with a small forest in the middle of the desert. You will soon reach a small roundabout directly in front of Bida bint Saud. Currently, there is no parking or real entrance and you must park at the side of the road and negotiate your way past concrete boulders, but with the pace of tourist developments in and near Al Ain, it is likely that there will soon be proper parking and an entrance.

A sign in front gives information about the site and if you make your way to the summit, you will see several restored structures which are collective tombs from the Iron Age, dated at approximately 1000 - 600 BC and you will get an excellent view of the stone heaps at the foot of the outcrop which are single chamber tombs from approximately 3000 BC. The summit also provides a view of camel enclosures and vegetable fields contrasted with red dunes.

DIRECTIONS TO BIDA BINT SAUD

1. Zero your odometer at the Sheikha Salama Mosque R/A you will be heading out of Al Ain towards the Dubai Road on Salahuddeen Al Ayyubi Street with the mosque on your right hand side.
2. At the next roundabout go straight continuing on Salahuddeen Al Ayyubi Street.
3. At the next roundabout (Globe R/A) turn left on Ali Ibn Abi Taleb Street.
4. At the next roundabout, Al Mandoos (Jewellery Box) R/A, turn right.
5. Drive along Al Ain Street to the next traffic lights, which is a T-junction and turn left onto Shakhboot Ibn Sultan Street.
6. At the next roundabout, the Zayed Library R/A with the UAE University on the opposite corner on your left, turn right.
7. Cross the bridge driving down Mohammad Ibn Khalifa Street.
8. Go straight through the next roundabout.
9. Go straight through the next roundabout.
10. Go straight through the next set of traffic lights. You can turn left here for Qattara Oasis.
11. Go straight through the next roundabout.
12. Go straight through the next roundabout.
13. Go straight through the next roundabout the Al Rumailah Roundabout. You can turn here for Hili Oasis.
14. Go straight through the next roundabout.
15. Go straight through the next roundabout the turning should be signposted to Bida bint Saud. You would turn right here for Dubai.
16. Go straight through the next roundabout.
17. Go straight past the turning for Nahil on the **E95**.
18. Duel-carriage way starts just before the next roundabout; go straight through it and take the road signposted Qarn bint Saud. The duel carriage ends.
19. The next roundabout is just in front of Bida bint Saud. Go left at the roundabout. Park on the side of the road near the entrance in the fence around Bida bint Saud. There is a dirt track around the perimeter which can be driven round, but beware of drifting sand.

BIDA BINT SAUD

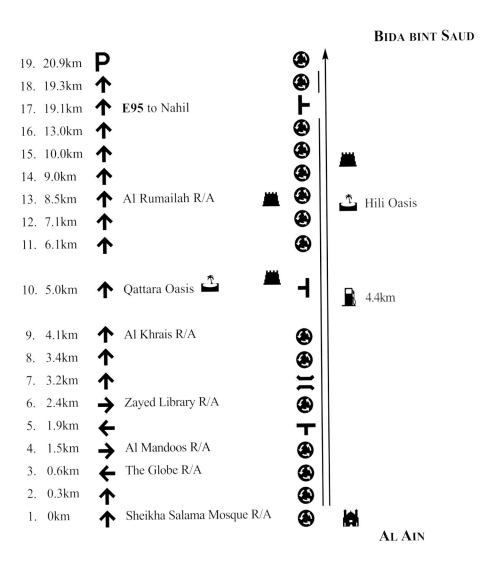

19.	20.9km	P
18.	19.3km	↑
17.	19.1km	↑ E95 to Nahil
16.	13.0km	↑
15.	10.0km	↑
14.	9.0km	↑
13.	8.5km	↑ Al Rumailah R/A
12.	7.1km	↑
11.	6.1km	↑
10.	5.0km	↑ Qattara Oasis
9.	4.1km	↑ Al Khrais R/A
8.	3.4km	↑
7.	3.2km	↑
6.	2.4km	→ Zayed Library R/A
5.	1.9km	←
4.	1.5km	→ Al Mandoos R/A
3.	0.6km	← The Globe R/A
2.	0.3km	↑
1.	0km	↑ Sheikha Salama Mosque R/A

Hili Oasis

4.4km

AL AIN

ROUTE KILOMETRES

STEP	ACTION	KM	DISTANCE KM	STEP	ACTION	KM	DISTANCE KM
10.	Go straight	5.0		19.	End	20.9	
			0.9				1.6
9.	Go straight	4.1		18.	Go straight	19.3	
			0.7				0.2
8.	Go straight	3.4		17.	Go straight	19.1	
			0.2				6.1
7.	Go straight	3.2		16.	Go straight	13.0	
			0.8				3.0
6.	Turn right	2.4		15.	Go straight	10.0	
			0.5				1.0
5.	Turn left	1.9		14.	Go straight	9.0	
			0.4				0.5
4.	Turn right	1.5		13.	Go straight	8.5	
			0.9				1.4
3.	Turn left	0.6		12.	Go straight	7.1	
			0.3				1.0
2.	Go straight	0.3		11.	Go straight	6.1	
			0.3				1.1
1.	Start	0					

AL AIN TO HATTA THROUGH OMAN

ROAD QUALITY	✔✔✔✔
SHADE/AMENITIES	✔✔✔
ACCESSIBILITY	✔✔✔✔✔
TIME TAKEN	✔✔✔
MY RATING	✔✔✔✔

STARTING POINT:	Al Ain, Sheikha Salama Mosque R/A in the town centre
FINISHING POINT:	Hatta Fort R/A
DISTANCE:	117.6km
ROAD CONDITIONS:	Good tarred road
THINGS TO SEE:	Rugged mountains and wadis
NOTES:	You are crossing into Oman, although you are not crossing a border post. Check that your UAE car insurance covers you here.

The route from Al Ain to Hatta is perhaps my favourite of all the routes in the book - a relaxing easy drive on excellent quiet roads through spectacular mountains. A recently completed upgraded tarred road now connects Buraimi to the E44, just above Hatta. This is a useful road as it makes for an easy drive between Buraimi and Hatta driving through the rugged mountains and across dry wadis. This is in contrast to using the E55, which is a more sand dune landscape. It also provides routes in and out of Hatta Pools without having to back track. The road rises and falls dramatically and crosses numerous wadi crossings. At any of these you might want to take a walk along the wadi where grasses, palms and low thorn trees flourish despite the lack of any visible water. All along the route are craggy outcrops of variegated hues from sandy-beige to black. Occasional hamlets and tiny date plantations dot the landscape. The numerous wadis, gullies and large fissures in the rocks occasionally transform into streams, rivers and even lakes and waterfalls after the sudden rains, but disappear just as mysteriously leaving only moulded rocks with fantastical shapes streaked with a rainbow of colours from the minerals and dripping water.

On the way, there is a turn-off to Al Rodha/Wadi Al Qahfi; which will take you on a dirt road all the way to the Hatta Pools, but this route has not been suggested as the dirt road has some steep and rocky descents and climbs. Just before you reach Hatta, you will find a charming series of stalls selling carpets and pottery. There you are likely, if you bargain effectively, to buy an inexpensive silk or wool carpet, or any number of pots in amazing shapes. I have even seen a pottery camel a metre and a half high! It's well worth it to spend some time in Hatta itself with its forts, Hatta Heritage Village with fascinating displays and the Hatta Fort Hotel where you can relax at the rock pool for a small fee after a hard day's driving.

DIRECTIONS AL AIN TO HATTA

1. Zero your odometer at the Sheikha Salama Mosque R/A. Drive down Salahuddeen Al Ayyubi Street with the mosque on your right hand side.
2. At next roundabout with Pizza Hut on the opposite corner turn right.
3. Drive straight down Khalifa Ibn Zayed Street to the next set of traffic lights and turn left onto Abu Baker Al Siddiq Street.
4. Turn right at the next roundabout signposted Mezyad.
5. Drive down Shakhboot Ibn Sultan Street to the next roundabout and go all the way round it until you are going the direction you just came from.
6. At the next set of traffic lights take the feed road to the right signposted to Buraimi. You will shortly cross the Oman border at the 'Peace be with you' sign.
7. Go straight across the bridge at 5.5km and another at 5.9km.
8. At the next roundabout Hesn R/A (Buraimi Souq) take the feed road to the right signposted Muscat / Salalah. Buraimi New Souq is on your left hand side.
9. Go straight to the next roundabout and turn left following the signpost to Al Khadra.
10. As you approach the next roundabout you will see a big mosque on the opposite side. Take the second road on your right signposted to Al Jizi/Sohar. Drive past the Buraimi Hotel on your left
11. Turn left at the next roundabout (Hospital R/A). The road is signposted to Mahdah. After about 2.5 kms you will come across the Buraimi Industrial Estate on your left. Continue straight on.
12. Further along this road, you will pass the sign to the sewerage works. This is the road to access Fossil Valley on your right.
13. Continue straight and turn left on the road for the Wadi Al Qahfi campsite. This turning is also signposted to Mahdah H.C. and Al Rodha.
14. Drive to the next roundabout and go straight through it to the road signposted to Al Juwaif.
15. About 4.5 km after the roundabout the road will dip down to cross a wadi.
16. 5.5km from the roundabout is the turning for Khadra on the right.
17. Continue past the Khadra turning and take the next left turning for Wadi Al Qahfi campsite. The road is also signposted to Al Rawdah. The road will continue crossing numerous wadis either dipping into them or crossing them by bridge.
18. You will pass the road to Hatta Pools signposted to Al Fay.
19. After driving through the mountains for 34.4km you will reach the **E44** with a Shell Petrol Station on the left. Turn right here for Hatta. The road into Hatta is lined with stalls on both sides selling carpets and clay pots. As well as the stalls, there are a number of petrol stations too.
20. After about 20km you will reach the Hatta Fort R/A. Here you can turn left for the Hatta Fort Hotel. Go straight on the main road to the Oman border crossing, or turn right and go into Hatta. It is the starting point for the Hatta Pools route page 65.

Al Ain to Hatta through Oman

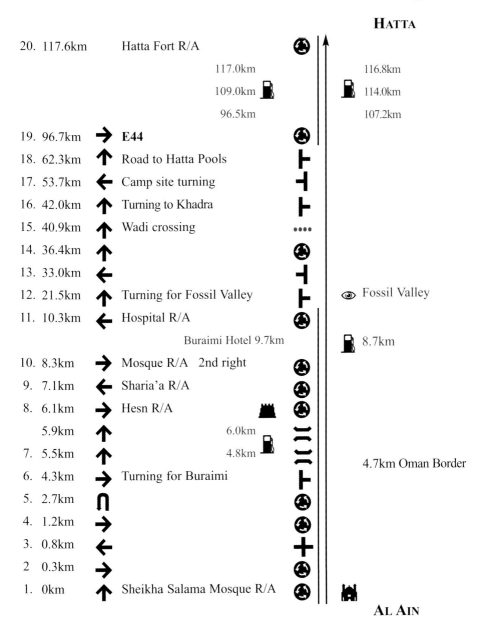

HATTA

20. 117.6km   Hatta Fort R/A

117.0km   116.8km
109.0km   114.0km
96.5km   107.2km

19. 96.7km   → **E44**
18. 62.3km   ↑ Road to Hatta Pools
17. 53.7km   ← Camp site turning
16. 42.0km   ↑ Turning to Khadra
15. 40.9km   ↑ Wadi crossing
14. 36.4km   ↑
13. 33.0km   ←
12. 21.5km   ↑ Turning for Fossil Valley   Fossil Valley
11. 10.3km   ← Hospital R/A

Buraimi Hotel 9.7km   8.7km

10. 8.3km   → Mosque R/A   2nd right
9. 7.1km   ← Sharia'a R/A
8. 6.1km   → Hesn R/A
    5.9km   ↑   6.0km
7. 5.5km   ↑   4.8km
6. 4.3km   → Turning for Buraimi   4.7km Oman Border
5. 2.7km   ∩
4. 1.2km   →
3. 0.8km   ←
2   0.3km   →
1. 0km   ↑ Sheikha Salama Mosque R/A

AL AIN

61

ROUTE KILOMETRES

STEP	ACTION	KM	DISTANCE KM	STEP	ACTION	KM	DISTANCE KM
			2.0	20.	End	117.6	
10.	2nd right	8.3					20.9
			1.2	19.	Turn right	96.7	
9.	Turn left	7.1					34.4
			1.0	18.	Go straight	62.3	
8.	Turn right	6.1					8.6
			0.6	17.	Turn left	53.7	
7.	Go straight	5.5					11.7
			1.2	16.	Go straight	42.0	
6.	Turn right	4.3					1.1
			1.6	15.	Go straight	40.9	
5.	U turn	2.7					4.5
			1.5	14.	Go straight	36.4	
4.	Turn right	1.2					3.4
			0.4	13.	Turn left	33.0	
3.	Turn left	0.8					11.5
			0.5	12.	Go straight	21.5	
2.	Turn right	0.3					11.2
			0.3	11.	Turn left	10.3	
1.	Start	0					

62

OTHER THINGS TO DO IN HATTA

Hatta is an interesting town to visit, especially if you are interested in the history of the UAE.

● The Hatta Heritage Village gives a good example of the kind of housing people lived in in the past. A hill tower has been restored so visitors can take advantage of the view. It also has reasonable toilets so provides for a good bathroom break.

● The Hatta Dam provides an interesting view of the oases and Hatta town as well as a pleasant drive.

HATTA TO HATTA POOLS

ROAD QUALITY	✔
SHADE/AMENITIES	✔
ACCESSIBILITY	✔✔
TIME TAKEN	✔✔
MY RATING	✔✔✔

STARTING POINT:	Hatta Fort R/A
FINISHING POINT:	Hatta Pools
DISTANCE:	17.8km
ROAD CONDITIONS:	Tarred road to Al Fay, then about 6km of dirt road, this should not be driven during or after rain. The dirt road can be quite corrugated.
THINGS TO SEE:	Hatta Pools and other pools along the route, aflaj system, good picnic spots, rugged mountains and interesting rock formations.
NOTES:	To reach the pools, an uneven walk is required. No shade at pools.

The route from Hatta to Hatta Pools is a must for any visitor as flowing fresh water is an extreme rarity in the UAE. Hatta is a small oasis town, in which green palm groves contrast with the rugged mountains. It is easily reached from Dubai, Abu Dhabi, Fujairah or Al Ain, so this would make a good day trip. The route meanders past the Hatta Heritage Village and out past a number of small date plantations and farms on to a dirt road. You should take particular care on this road as it can be steep and a little rocky in places, but easily accessible by sedan car. Also, beware of goats that can saunter confidently across the road at any time.

On the way to the pools, you will find the delightful hamlet of Al Qarbi A'Sharqiyah. If you walk along the wadi you will find several small pools and shady trees ideal for a picnic or a quick paddle. This side trip is particularly useful as there is little or no shade at Hatta Pools. Shortly after Al Qarbi A'Sharqiyah, you will find the turn-off to Hatta Pools. You drive along side a falaj channel and cross over it before you find a parking area with a large metal dustbin - a kindly hint to visitors on where they should dispose of their litter. Follow the path down into the wadi and you will find several large pools in which you can paddle and even swim. The pools incredibly never dry up and remain deep throughout the summer and even years with no rain.

DIRECTIONS TO HATTA POOLS

1. This route starts at the end of the Dubai to Hatta route page 142 and the end of the Al Ain Hatta Route page 59. Zero your odometer at the Hatta Fort R/A. If coming from Dubai on the E44 turn right at the roundabout heading into Hatta Village.
2. Cross the bridge.
3. Go straight past the turning on your left.
4. After 2.6km, take the turning on the left to the Hatta Heritage Village.
5. Drive past the Heritage Village and turn left at the next roundabout.
6. Go straight past the turning on your right.
7. Cross the bridge.
8. Drive down the road and turn right onto the road to Al Fay. You will see flags painted on the hill just beyond the turning.
9. Drive along this road crossing a bridge and then crossing the Oman border.
10. Go straight across the bridge.
11. Just outside Al Fay the tar comes to an end and you turn right onto a dirt road, signposted to Wadi Al Qahfi Camp site.
12. Drive along the road for 4.7km and you have reached the turn off for the side trip.
13. Continue along the road for 1.3km till you reach the turn off for Hatta Pools. You can go straight on to Ray and then on to Al Ain or loop back to Hatta.
14. The turn off road appears to turn back on the road you have just travelled. Follow it for 0.6km till you reach a parking spot above the Hatta Pools. The pools cannot be seen from the parking spot and a 500-metre walk will be required to get to the pools.

HATTA POOLS

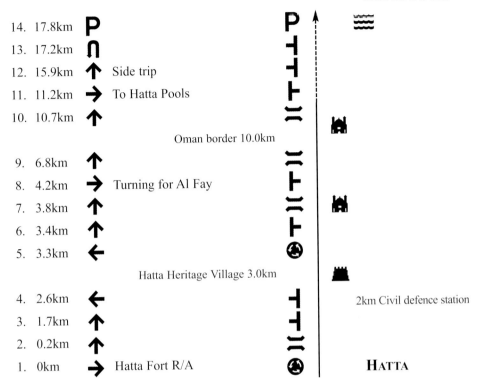

14. 17.8km
13. 17.2km
12. 15.9km Side trip
11. 11.2km To Hatta Pools
10. 10.7km

Oman border 10.0km

9. 6.8km
8. 4.2km Turning for Al Fay
7. 3.8km
6. 3.4km
5. 3.3km

Hatta Heritage Village 3.0km

4. 2.6km
3. 1.7km
2. 0.2km
1. 0km Hatta Fort R/A

2km Civil defence station

HATTA

ROUTE KILOMETRES

STEP	ACTION	KM	DISTANCE KM	STEP	ACTION	KM	DISTANCE KM
			0.4	14.	End	17.8	
7.	Go straight	3.8		13.	Turn left	17.2	0.6
			1.2				
6.	Go straight	3.4		12.	Go straight	15.9	1.3
			0.1				
5.	Turn left	3.3		11.	Turn right	11.2	4.7
			0.7				
4.	Turn left	2.6		10.	Go straight	10.7	0.5
			0.9				
3.	Go straight	1.7		9.	Go straight	6.8	1.9
			1.5				
2.	Go straight	0.2		8.	Turn right	4.2	2.6
			0.2				
1.	Start	0					

SIDE TRIP - HATTA POOLS

You cannot see Hatta Pools from where you have parked your car, as they are down in the wadi. The only water you can see at the car park is a falaj channel snaking along the side of the road. A track runs down from the car park to the pools. It first drops into a flatter area, which has been used for camping, then up over a rise to the wadi proper. From here you will see the pools. There is no shade here other than that you can obtain from the wadi sides. It is well worth going for a walk up and down the wadi exploring the various pools the water flows into and the waterfalls as the water flows over the rocks.

SIDE TRIP - AL QARBI A'SHARQIYAH

Just before reaching the pools, one can turn down one of the side roads at 15.9km or just over the hump at 16km (the second road is better) it is signposted to Al Qarbi A'Sharqiyah. After 0.1km the two roads meet and continue as one at 0.3 km. Drive up the path to the village and you will find a small dam with tiny fishes. Please do not swim in this as it provides a water supply for irrigation and drinking water. There is a building on your right and on your left is a dam walled with stones. The pool created is full of fish. Flowing from the pool is a falaj channel that follows the road. Continue on the road which goes away from the wadi round a hill. At 0.6km, the road forks, take the left fork again at 0.7km. The road then crosses a bridge across a wadi and goes up the side of the wadi to the village of Al Qarbi A'Sharqiyah. There is a clearing here where you can park. If you go back down to the wadi and across the bridge and walk down stream, after about 500 metres on your left, you can walk down to some pools that have shade from a mango tree and the steep wadi walls. This is a great spot for a picnic and to soak your feet.

DRIVING ON FROM THE POOLS TO AL AIN

The road to Hatta Pools continues on to Al Fay and then joins the road used in the AL AIN TO HATTA route page 59. One can either use that road to go onto Buraimi then Al Ain or to go back to Hatta. I do advise caution for the faint-hearted as there are some steep climbs and descents that a small-engine car may find difficult. The road is also very rutted, thus it produces a rather vibrating ride that some may find a good test of their car's fittings. Additionally there are a number of wadi crossings, thus this should not be attempted after rain. However, if you feel your car is up to it, it is a good drive. There are also a number of good pools near some of the wadi crossings on the route.

HATTA TO FUJAIRAH

ROAD QUALITY	✔✔✔✔
SHADE/AMENITIES	✔✔✔
ACCESSIBILITY	✔✔✔✔
TIME TAKEN	✔✔✔
MY RATING	✔✔✔

STARTING POINT:	Hatta Fort R/A
FINISHING POINT:	Fujairah
DISTANCE:	64.2km
ROAD CONDITIONS:	Good tarred road
THINGS TO SEE:	Rugged mountains and interesting rock formations, tunnel through the mountains
NOTES:	The route links up with other east coast routes.

The route from Hatta to Fujairah is useful as it links Hatta to the East Coast through the mountains. The route joins with the Sharjah to Khor Kalba route at Munay, page 93. Then, it joins the route to Al Ghamour page 87 and you can also turn off the route to meet up with the route to Wadi Al Hayl Palace page 83. Finally, it joins the **E89** on the route from Masafi to Fujairah page 77 as you enter Fujairah. This pleasant route which twists its way through the mountains provides a great link to the East Coast from Hatta, enabling you to discover the UAE without too much back tracking.

In addition, instead of following the route to Munay from the Huwaylat roundabout, you can take a side-trip, turning right at the roundabout and driving down a road to the Oman border. This provides a view of small villages and farms and, if you look carefully, you will see watchtowers and fort ruins on the surrounding hills. The road from Hatta to Huwaylat weaving its way up and down through the mountains provides a number of spots to pull off and take a break under a bush or, for the more adventurous, to camp. The dramatic mountains provide an interesting backdrop to the trip, although they are somewhat marred by the abundance of gravity-defying powerlines criss-crossing the route.

DIRECTIONS TO FUJAIRAH

1.   This route starts at the end of the Dubai to Hatta route page 142 and the end of the Al Ain Hatta Route page 59. Zero your odometer at the Hatta Fort R/A. If coming from Dubai on the **E44** go straight at the roundabout heading to the Oman border.

2.   After less than 1km turn left onto a road heading into the mountains signposted Huwaylat Munay.

3.   At 11.4 km you should reach the Huwaylat roundabout turn left following the sign to Ras Al Khaimah. You can turn right here to do the side trip to see the fort ruins.

4.   Turn right at the roundabout onto the road to Khor Kalba used in the Sharjah to Khor Kalba route page 93. If you go straight then turn left at the next roundabout you will be on the road to Sharjah and Dubai.

5.   Go through the tunnel.

6.   Turn right onto the feed road.

7.   Turn left. This is the road used in the Fujairah Al Ghamour route page 87. If you turn right you will be heading to Al Ghamour.

8.   Go straight past the turning for Sharjah.

9.   Turn left at the T-junction. Turning right will take you to Kalba.

10.   Go straight through the roundabout. Turning left will take you to another roundabout, which is on the Fujairah to Wadi Al Hayl Palace route page 83.

11.   The road will come to an end forcing you to turn left.

12.   Turn right.

13.-17.   Cross 5 bridges.

18.   Turn right onto the **E89** heading into Fujairah. Turning left will take you to Masafi. You have now joined the Masafi to Fujairah route page 77.

19.   The route ends at the big oval roundabout in Fujairah. Here you can decide to go into Fujairah or to head up to Dibba along the East Coast.

FUJAIRAH

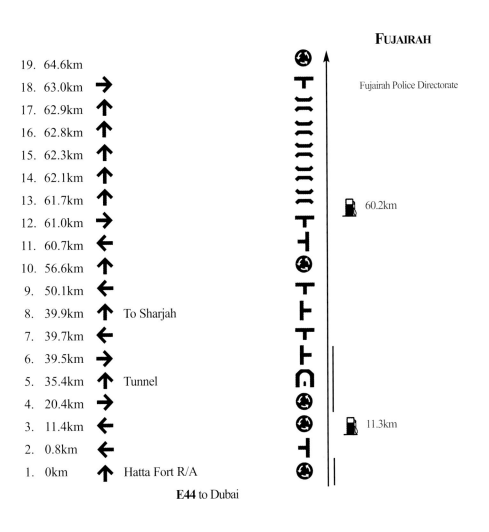

Fujairah Police Directorate

19.	64.6km	
18.	63.0km →	
17.	62.9km ↑	
16.	62.8km ↑	
15.	62.3km ↑	
14.	62.1km ↑	
13.	61.7km ↑	
12.	61.0km →	
11.	60.7km ←	
10.	56.6km ↑	
9.	50.1km ←	
8.	39.9km ↑	To Sharjah
7.	39.7km ←	
6.	39.5km →	
5.	35.4km ↑	Tunnel
4.	20.4km →	
3.	11.4km ←	
2.	0.8km ←	
1.	0km ↑	Hatta Fort R/A

60.2km

11.3km

E44 to Dubai

HATTA

73

ROUTE KILOMETRES

STEP	ACTION	KM	DISTANCE KM	STEP	ACTION	KM	DISTANCE KM
10.	Go straight	56.6		19.	End	64.6	
			6.5				1.5
9.	Turn left	50.1		18.	Go straight	63.0	
			10.2				0.1
8.	Go straight	39.9		17.	Go straight	62.9	
			0.2				0.1
7.	Turn left	39.7		16.	Go straight	62.8	
			0.2				0.5
6.	Turn right	39.5		15.	Go straight	62.3	
			4.1				0.2
5.	Go straight	35.4		14.	Go straight	62.1	
			14.7				0.4
4.	Turn right	20.4		13.	Go straight	61.7	
			1.0				0.7
3.	Turn left	11.4		12.	Turn right	61.0	
			0.6				0.4
2.	Turn left	0.8		11.	Turn left	60.7	
			0.8				4.0
1.	Start	0					

SIDE TRIP - HUWAYLAT

Turn right at the Huwaylat Roundabout (step 3 on page 72 & 73). Drive down this road looking at the oasis on the side of the road as well as ruined watchtowers and forts. After 12.5km the road will turn to gravel and shortly after that you will reach the checkpoint for crossing into Oman. Watch out for the speed bumps on this road.

MASAFI TO FUJAIRAH

ROAD QUALITY	✔✔✔✔
SHADE/AMENITIES	✔✔✔
ACCESSIBILITY	✔✔✔✔✔
TIME TAKEN	✔✔
MY RATING	✔✔✔

STARTING POINT:	Masafi R/A
FINISHING POINT:	Fujairah
DISTANCE:	32.4km
ROAD CONDITIONS:	Very good tarred road
THINGS TO SEE:	Mountains and deep wadis, forts and the Gulf of Oman
NOTES:	This can be a busy road with trucks going slowly up the hills

The route from Masafi to Fujairah cuts through the jagged mountains to the increasingly popular palm-fringed city of Fujairah: a get away for city-dwellers from Dubai and Abu Dhabi and a gateway to the East coast and the Gulf of Oman. This route starts at the end of the Dubai to Masafi route (page 148). It also links up with the route from Khor Kalba to Dibba (page 99). The Dibba to Al Dhaid route (page 111) also crosses this starting point. If you are inclined, you could make a triangle trip, taking in the full spectrum of the East coast, driving from Masafi to Fujairah then to Dibba and from Dibba back to Masafi. Once again, this route showcases awe-inspiring mountains and dramatic drops into canyons. Near the turn-off to Daftah, the mountains loom so claustrophobically close to the road that they appear ready to stride across it and engulf the motorist. Gardens and oases cling to the cliffs near Blaydah and the fort at Bithnah, which dates from 1735, could make an interesting side trip. Finally, the route culminates in Fujairah itself with its incongruous high buildings contrasting with the rugged mountains behind.

Along with tourism, the city is also a rapidly developing commercial centre. Its strategic location, which provides easy access to international shipping routes, has played a key role in its development as one of the world's top oil-bunkering ports, although the traditional mainstays of the economy, fishing and agriculture, are obviously still prominent. In Fujairah, the route passes the Fujairah Fort or Castle as it is more popularly known and Fujairah Museum. The castle was built in 1670 and lies on a small hill close to date plantations. The castle consists of three major parts, several halls and towers. It was damaged by British bombardment in the early twentieth century, but was extensively renovated in 2000 and the renovation is ongoing. The museum, which is just south of the fort and opposite the ruler's palace, houses many of the artefacts found in archaeological digs at Qidfah, Bithnah and Wadi Al Hayl.

77

DIRECTIONS TO FUJAIRAH

1.   This route starts at the end of the feeder route from Dubai to
      Masafi page 148. Zero your kilometres at the roundabout and take
      the turning to Fujairah. From this roundabout you can also take the
      road to Dibba as used by the Dibba to Al Dhaid route page 111.
2.   Go across the bridge.
3.   Go across the bridge.
4.   Go across the bridge.
5.   Go straight past the turning for Daftah.
6.   Go across the bridge.
7.   Go across the bridge.
8.   Go past the turning for Blaydah.
9.   Go past the turning for Bithnah. Bithnah has an old fort that is
      worth a look but there are better forts around Fujairah.
10.   Go across the bridge.
11.   Go past the turning for the reservoir.
12.   Go across the bridge.
13.   Go across the bridge.
14.   Go across the bridge.
15.   Go straight past the turning on your right signposted for Forensic
      Science Lab. This is the starting point for the routes to Al Ghamour
      and the Hayl Palace on pages 87 and 83. Shortly after this
      turning you will pass the Fujairah Police Directorate on your left.
16.   Take the third turning on the big oval roundabout. Signposted to
      Madhab and Al Ittihad **E17**. Taking the second turning will take
      you into the town centre.
17.   Go straight at the next roundabout.
18.   At the next roundabout take the second turning.
19.   Go straight past the turning on your left for Fujairah Museum and
      fort. You can take this turning to drive down a dirt road to the
      museum and get close to the fort and surrounding ruins.
20.   Turn left at the next roundabout. Old Sheikh Palace R/A.
21.   The route ends at the Coffee Pot Roundabout. Here you can turn
      left to join up with the **E99** to go along the Coast to Dibba as in the
      route to Dibba on page 99 or turn right to Khor Kalba.

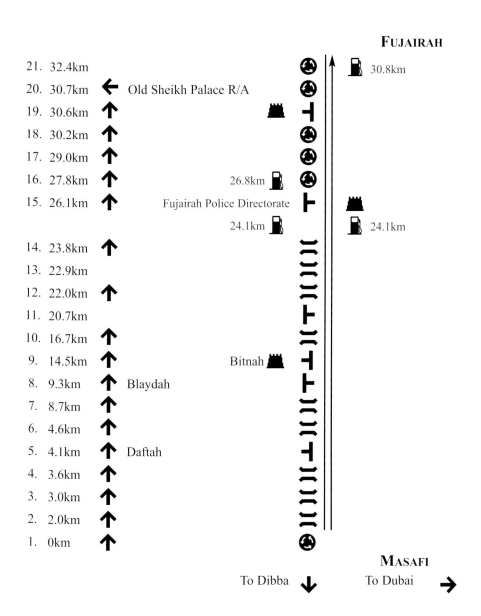

FUJAIRAH

21. 32.4km   30.8km

20. 30.7km ← Old Sheikh Palace R/A

19. 30.6km ↑

18. 30.2km ↑

17. 29.0km ↑

16. 27.8km ↑   26.8km

15. 26.1km ↑   Fujairah Police Directorate

           24.1km   24.1km

14. 23.8km ↑

13. 22.9km

12. 22.0km ↑

11. 20.7km

10. 16.7km ↑

9. 14.5km ↑   Bitnah

8. 9.3km ↑ Blaydah

7. 8.7km ↑

6. 4.6km ↑

5. 4.1km ↑ Daftah

4. 3.6km ↑

3. 3.0km ↑

2. 2.0km ↑

1. 0km ↑

MASAFI

To Dibba ↓   To Dubai →

79

Masafi to Fujairah

ROUTE KILOMETRES

Step	Action	KM	Distance km	Step	Action	KM	Distance km
11.	Go straight	20.7		21.	End	32.4	
			4.0				1.7
10.	Go straight	16.7		20.	Turn left	30.7	
			2.2				0.1
9.	Go straight	14.5		19.	Go straight	30.6	
			5.2				0.4
8.	Go straight	9.3		18.	Go straight	30.2	
			0.6				1.2
7.	Go straight	8.7		17.	Go straight	29.0	
			4.1				1.2
6.	Go straight	4.6		16.	Go straight	27.8	
			0.5				1.7
5.	Go straight	4.1		15.	Go straight	26.1	
			0.5				2.3
4.	Go straight	3.6		14.	Go straight	23.8	
			0.6				0.9
3.	Go straight	3.0		13.	Go straight	22.9	
			1.0				0.9
2.	Go straight	2.0		12.	Go straight	22.0	
			2.0				1.3
1.	Start	0					

OTHER THINGS TO DO IN FUJAIRAH

Fujairah, located on the Indian Ocean coast, is struggling with the competing interests of its role as a shipping port frequented by tankers and as a tourist escape. Large areas of date plantations make this a green and inviting city. With the full range of restaurants and hotels it is a good place for the traveller to take a break and refuel. Here are some of the other attractions Fujairah has to offer:

● Bullfights, bull against bull, are held on Fridays in winter 4pm near the palm groves off the Kalba/Oman road.
● The Fujairah Museum contains impressive exhibits from the past.
● Ain Al Madhab Gardens house mineral baths fed by mineral springs.
● The Fujairah Fort is an impressive structure set against the mountains.

81

Fujairah to Wadi Al Hayl Palace

ROAD QUALITY	✔✔✔
SHADE/AMENITIES	✔✔✔
ACCESSIBILITY	✔✔✔
TIME TAKEN	✔
MY RATING	✔✔✔✔

STARTING POINT:	Opposite, after Fujairah Police Station
FINISHING POINT:	Wadi Al Hayl Palace
DISTANCE:	10.1km
ROAD CONDITIONS:	Very good tarred road
THINGS TO SEE:	The palace ruins, petroglyphs, mountains, oases and wadis.
NOTES:	Wadi bashing without the bash

Outside Fujairah, immediately after the police station, an unassuming turnoff takes you into the mountains. This short route starts out urbanely with single carriageway quickly becoming shiny new dual carriageway. However, the dual carriageway soon reverts to single about four kilometres along the route. Then, the route wends its way through the new village of Al Hayl, along the wadi floor between steep wadi walls and you enjoy a wadi-bash without bashing, except for the numerous speed bumps in the village. Finally, you reach the site of the old village of Al Hayl which consists of a number of different buildings in varying states of repair scattered about the sides and terraces of the main wadi and its tributaries. Archaeologists have recently carbon dated the small fort or 'hisn' which sits protectively on top of a small rock outcrop dated between 1470 and 1700 AD. The building features loopholes and firing slots.

Just below the fort are more modern remains consisting of the palace of Sheikh Abdullah bin Hamdan Al Sharqi, houses, field walls and a cemetery dating from the beginning of the 20th century. The palace itself consists of an enclosed compound containing meeting rooms, storerooms, bedrooms and a kitchen. You can continue along the dirt road following the wadi after the palace and discover more stone wall ruins. If you make your way down to the wadi below and look carefully, you will see petroglyphs, or pictures engraved on stone on either side of the wadi. Many of these depict animals or horses and riders probably dating back to the early 1st or 2nd millennium BC. This route provides all the pleasures we have come to expect from off-road driving, but entirely on tarmac.

DIRECTIONS TO WADI AL HAYL PALACE

1.   This route starts on the road out of Fujairah to Masafi the **E89**, just past Fujairah Police Station, on the opposite side of the road. The turnoff is marked on the Masafi to Fujairah route on page 77.

2.-6.   Just after the turning, you will cross 5 small bridges in quick succession.

7.   Go straight through the roundabout following the sign to Al Hayl. An army camp is on your right

8.   Go straight through the roundabout following the sign to Al Hayl. Turning left will take you to Ain Al Ghamour page 87.

9.   You will pass through the village of Al Hayl and over a number of speed bumps. The road then heads into and along the wadi. The road steeply climbs up the side of the wadi to a viewing area above a dam.

10.   You will have reached the end of the tarmac and be at the front of the palace ruins. You can drive on a bit on the dirt road round the side of the palace find a place to park then explore the ruins and wadi below.

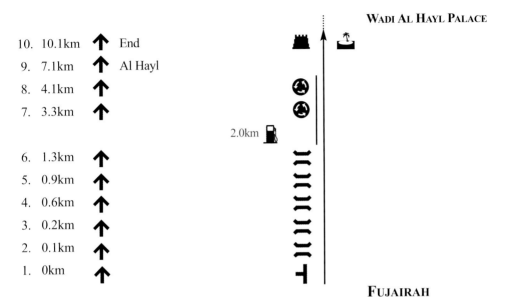

10. 10.1km ↑ End
9. 7.1km   ↑ Al Hayl
8. 4.1km   ↑
7. 3.3km   ↑

6. 1.3km   ↑
5. 0.9km   ↑
4. 0.6km   ↑
3. 0.2km   ↑
2. 0.1km   ↑
1. 0km   ↑

WADI AL HAYL PALACE

2.0km

FUJAIRAH

ROUTE KILOMETRES

STEP	ACTION	KM	DISTANCE KM	STEP	ACTION	KM	DISTANCE KM
5.	Go straight	0.9		10.	End	10.1	
			0.3				3.0
4.	Go straight	0.6		9.	Go straight	7.1	
			0.4				3.0
3.	Go straight	0.2		8.	Go straight	4.1	
			0.1				0.8
2.	Go straight	0.1		7.	Go straight	3.3	
			0.1				2.1
1.	Start	0		6.	Go straight	1.3	
							0.4

85

FUJAIRAH TO AL GHAMOUR

ROAD QUALITY	✔✔✔✔
SHADE/AMENITIES	✔✔✔
ACCESSIBILITY	✔✔✔
TIME TAKEN	✔✔
MY RATING	✔✔✔✔

STARTING POINT:	Opposite, just past the Fujairah Police Station
FINISHING POINT:	Al Ghamour
DISTANCE:	41.5km
ROAD CONDITIONS:	Very good tarred road all the way
THINGS TO SEE:	Mountains and deep wadis, forts
NOTES:	Al Ghamour has dried up a bit and needs rain

Before the new village of Al Hayl, a road to the left cuts its way into the steep mountains. The route winds through newly scarred rock and it feels as if the deserted, but beautifully built road has been constructed just for you, as the silence is almost eerie between the black rock and deep gullies. Sleepy hamlets and small oases dot the landscape and soon the vista widens to an open plain to your left with numerous thorn trees. The landscape appears almost like an Africa savannah, although the 'big two' you see are goats and donkeys, rather than lions or buffalo! In the small village of Ohala, a tarmac turnoff quickly reverts to dirt and three hundred metres from the main road you will see the Ohala Fort, which is currently in the process of renovation. The fort overlooks a wadi and small oasis.

Finally, the route reaches the picnic spot of Ain Al Ghamour. Although the shelters are a little dilapidated and the hot springs have all but dried up as a result of recent hot dry summers, the area is still one of great natural beauty only slightly scarred by humans. Lush plant growth indicates underground water and locals, most especially Omanis from just over the border, love to picnic here and make use of the curative waters which can reach 60°C. It is said to cure diseases like rheumatism and arthritis, even though they nowadays have to resort to using buckets to dispense small amounts of the water from a tank, rather than fully bathing in the water as of yore.

DIRECTIONS TO AIN AL GHAMOUR

1. This route starts on the road out of Fujairah to Masafi the **E89**, just past Fujairah Police Station, on the opposite side of the road. The turnoff is marked on the Masafi to Fujairah route on page 77.

2.- 6. Just after the turning you will cross 5 small bridges in quick succession.

7. Go straight through the roundabout following the sign to Al Hayl. An army camp is on your right

8. Turn left at the roundabout following the sign to Ain Al Ghamour. Going straight will take you to Wadi Hayl Palace page 83.

9. At the next roundabout turn right following the sign to Ain Al Ghamour.

10. Turn right following the sign to Ain Al Ghamour.

11. Go straight past the turning to Wadi Mai.

12. Go straight past the turning on your left. It will take you to Sharjah via Meliha or turn off at Munay for Hatta the road used in the Hatta to Fujairah route page 71.

13. Go straight under the bridge.

14. Go straight past the turning on your right. It will take you to Khor Kalba and is the road used for the Sharjah to Khor Kalba Mangroves route page 93.

15. Go straight past the turning for Wadi Hilo.

16. Go straight past Ohala. However it is well worth turning into Ohala to see the fort currently being restored that overlooks the wadi below.

17. Go straight across the bridge.

18. Turn left at the roundabout. Turning right would take you to Oman.

19. You will reach an open tarmac area. You can park here and walk to Ain Al Ghamour.

20. Turn onto the single lane dirt road to drive up to Ain Al Ghamour.

AL GHAMOUR

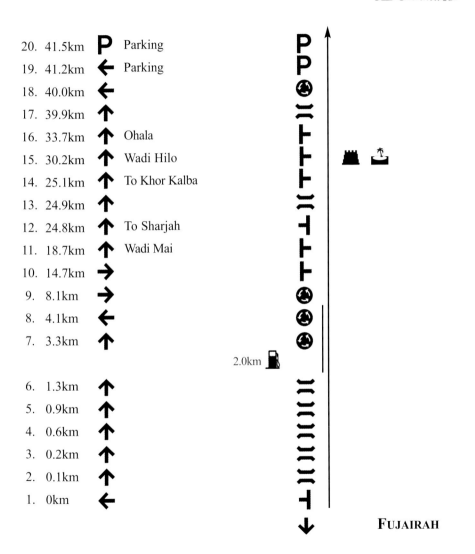

20.	41.5km	Parking
19.	41.2km	Parking
18.	40.0km	
17.	39.9km	
16.	33.7km	Ohala
15.	30.2km	Wadi Hilo
14.	25.1km	To Khor Kalba
13.	24.9km	
12.	24.8km	To Sharjah
11.	18.7km	Wadi Mai
10.	14.7km	
9.	8.1km	
8.	4.1km	
7.	3.3km	
	2.0km	
6.	1.3km	
5.	0.9km	
4.	0.6km	
3.	0.2km	
2.	0.1km	
1.	0km	

FUJAIRAH

Fujairah to Al Ghamour   　　　　　　　　　　　　　*On-Road in the UAE*

ROUTE KILOMETRES

STEP	ACTION	KM	DISTANCE KM	STEP	ACTION	KM	DISTANCE KM
			4.0	20.	End	41.5	
10.	Turn right	14.7					0.3
			6.6	19.	Turn left	41.2	
9.	Turn right	8.1					1.2
			4.0	18.	Turn left	40.0	
8.	Turn left	4.1					0.1
			0.8	17.	Go straight	39.9	
7.	Go straight	3.3					6.2
			2.0	16.	Go straight	33.7	
6.	Go straight	1.3					3.5
			0.4	15.	Go straight	30.2	
5.	Go straight	0.9					5.1
			0.3	14.	Go straight	25.1	
4.	Go straight	0.6					0.2
			0.4	13.	Go straight	24.9	
3.	Turn right	0.2					0.1
			0.1	12.	Go straight	24.8	
2.	Go straight	0.1					6.1
			0.1	11.	Go straight	18.7	
1.	Start	0					

SHARJAH TO KHOR KALBA MANGROVES

ROAD QUALITY	✔✔✔
SHADE/AMENITIES	✔✔✔
ACCESSIBILITY	✔✔✔✔✔
TIME TAKEN	✔✔✔
MY RATING	✔✔✔✔✔

STARTING POINT:	Sharjah
FINISHING POINT:	Khor Kalba Mangroves
DISTANCE:	108.7km
ROAD CONDITIONS:	Tarred road to mangroves, short dirt road to mangroves lagoon and beach
THINGS TO SEE:	Mountains, mangroves, Indian Ocean and birds
NOTES:	As the road was being widened at the time of writing, the road works may slightly affect the route as the duel carriageway is added through the mountains

This is a spectacular, but easy drive through the mountains to the mangroves and beach at Khor Kalba. After a dash through the desert on a new expressway, you quickly reach looming mountains, although you must avoid camels on the way. The road then twists its way up, down and through the mountains. The road goes into a 1.3km tunnel through a mountain then 12km later a shorter tunnel and you emerge on the other side with views down to the mangroves and out to the Indian Ocean (Gulf of Oman). The road twists its way steeply down to the ocean where you come across the rapidly developing outer suburbs of Khor Kalba. After negotiating your way through the suburbs, you hit the beach and if you drive along the beach, you will come to the mangroves.

A bridge has been constructed allowing you to cross the inlet and drive up to the edge of the mangroves and on to the beach. This is a good spot for swimming, sailing a dinghy or for a picnic, though you will need to bring your own shade. Bird watchers will enjoy the multitude of birds attracted to the mangroves and a possible chance to see the rare and only resident kingfisher native to the UAE the White-Collared Kingfisher.

The Kalba road S112 starts at the roundabout off the **E311** (Emirates Road). There is a flyover over the roundabout and National Paints is prominently advertised on a building near the roundabout. If you are coming down the **E311**, it is the junction after Interchange 1. Turn right and you will pass Sharjah University City on your left and after about 15km you will reach **E611** crossing the road. Start this route here. You can avoid some of the traffic by reaching the start of this route via the **E611**.

93

DIRECTIONS TO KHOR KALBA MANGROVES

1. Zero your odometer where the **E611** (Dubai Bypass road) joins the Kalba Road. The Meliha Road starts at the National Paints Roundabout in Sharjah. It is signposted from the **E611** as the turn off for Sharjah University, although you will be heading in the opposite direction from Sharjah. The Dubai to Masafi route page 148 crosses this starting point.
2. Go straight past the feed road on your right.
3. After travelling through the desert for 29km, you will pass through a step V-cutting in the hill ridge.
4. Go straight past the feed road on your right. It can be taken for Meliha or Al Dhaid. There is a petrol station in Meliha.
5. The road will now pass under the **E55** this is the turn off for Meliha. Continue straight. The mountains will start to appear ahead of you. At the point of writing, the road through the mountains was being widened from single lane to duel carriageway.
6. Go straight past the turn off for Munay. This road would take you to Hatta and it is the road used in the Hatta to Fujairah route page 71.
7. Go straight over the Flyover.
8. You go through the mountain in a 1.3km long 2-lane tunnel. After the tunnel the road is steep and twisty.
9. Go straight past the turning. The turning is for a road to Fujairah and the road used in the route to Al Ghamour page 87.
10. Go straight across the bridge.
11. You enter another shorter tunnel. When you emerge from the tunnel you have a good view out to sea. The road here is steep and twisty as it winds its way down to the coast.
12. Turn left at the next roundabout. Turning right will take you to the Oman border. They are developing a lagoon on your right.
13. Go straight through the next roundabout. Turning right here will take you to the roundabout at step 18, a short cut to the mangroves.
14. Go straight through the next roundabout.
15. At the next roundabout, turn right.
16. Go straight through the next roundabout.
17. Go straight through the next roundabout.
18. Turn right onto a duel carriageway road that runs along the beach, Corniche Street.
19. At the next roundabout, go straight ahead along the waters edge. There is a mosque on your right and just past the mosque is the Breeze Motel.
20. Turn left at the roundabout onto a dirt track.
21. Cross the single lane bridge ahead of you.
22. On your right you will see a children's playground and beyond that the mangroves.
23. Follow the track straight ahead bearing to the left to get to the beach. This is a hard track that a car can drive on when dry as you near the beach. Just be careful not to drive into any soft sand.

KHOR KALBA

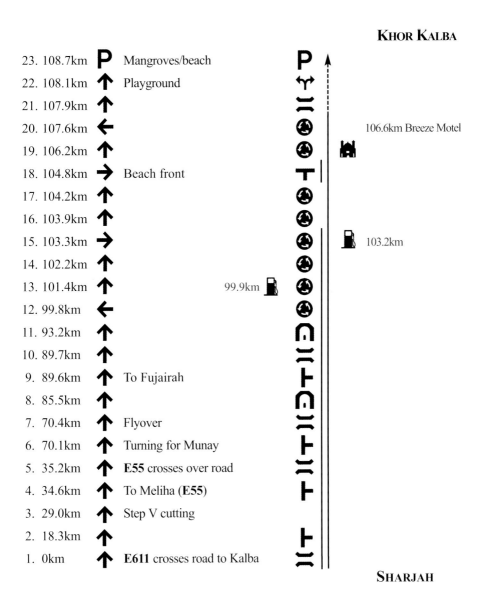

23. 108.7km   Mangroves/beach
22. 108.1km   Playground
21. 107.9km
20. 107.6km
19. 106.2km   106.6km Breeze Motel
18. 104.8km   Beach front
17. 104.2km
16. 103.9km
15. 103.3km   103.2km
14. 102.2km
13. 101.4km   99.9km
12. 99.8km
11. 93.2km
10. 89.7km
9. 89.6km   To Fujairah
8. 85.5km
7. 70.4km   Flyover
6. 70.1km   Turning for Munay
5. 35.2km   **E55** crosses over road
4. 34.6km   To Meliha (**E55**)
3. 29.0km   Step V cutting
2. 18.3km
1. 0km   **E611** crosses road to Kalba

SHARJAH

ROUTE KILOMETRES

STEP	ACTION	KM	DISTANCE KM	STEP	ACTION	KM	DISTANCE KM
12.	Turn left	99.8		23.	End	108.7	
			3.6				0.5
11.	Go straight	93.2		22.	Go straight	108.1	
			3.5				0.2
10.	Go straight	89.7		21.	Go straight	107.9	
			0.1				0.3
9.	Go straight	89.6		20.	Turn left	107.6	
			4.1				1.4
8.	Go straight	85.5		19.	Go straight	106.2	
			15.1				1.4
7.	Go straight	70.4		18.	Turn right	104.8	
			0.3				0.6
6.	Go straight	70.1		17.	Go straight	104.2	
			34.8				0.3
5.	Go straight	35.2		16.	Go straight	103.9	
			0.6				0.6
4.	Go straight	34.6		15.	Turn right	103.3	
			5.6				1.1
3.	Go straight	29.0		14.	Go straight	102.2	
			10.7				0.8
2.	Go straight	18.3		13.	Go straight	101.4	
			18.3				1.6
1.	Start	0					

KHOR KALBA TO DIBBA

ROAD QUALITY	✔✔✔✔
SHADE/AMENITIES	✔✔✔
ACCESSIBILITY	✔✔✔✔
TIME TAKEN	✔✔✔
MY RATING	✔✔✔

STARTING POINT:	Khor Kalba Mangroves
FINISHING POINT:	Dibba
DISTANCE:	76.4km
ROAD CONDITIONS:	Very good tarred road all the way
THINGS TO SEE:	East coast beaches, old mosque and forts
NOTES:	Non Muslims should not enter mosques

This is a drive along the beaches of the East Coast of the UAE. The road runs along the narrow stretch of land sandwiched between the sea and the mountains. Water from springs in the mountains turns the dry land green, creating stunning views. As you drive over headlands, you are presented with date and mango plantations set against the dark mountains and the blue sea. The Gulf of Oman is known for its good diving and some diving outfits have set up business in the small towns before you reach Dibba. There are pleasant beaches to stop at for a swim or picnic; some of them along this route have parks with grass and trees.

Halfway along the route, you will reach the small town of Al Bidayah which houses the Al Bidayah Mosque dated from 1446AD. This is not only one of the oldest surviving mosques in the Gulf, but also an unusual mosque due to its architecture. Instead of the usual one dome and minaret tower(s), this mosque has four pointed domes.

DIRECTIONS TO DIBBA

1.   This route starts at the bridge across to the mangroves at Khor Kalba. Zero your odometer here.
2.   At the roundabout, turn right.
3.   Pass the Breeze Motel and go straight through, bearing right at the next roundabout. You will be following the coast road along the beach.
4.   Go straight through the next roundabout.
5.   Go straight across the bridge.
6.   Go straight round the next roundabout. The beach along here has been lined with grass and trees.
7.   Go straight across the bridge.
8.   Go straight through the next roundabout.
9.   Go straight across the bridge.
10. Go straight through the next roundabout following the sign to Al Gurfa.
11. Go straight through the next roundabout.
12. Turn right at the next roundabout following the signs to Dibba on the **E99**.
13. Go straight through the next roundabout with the Fujairah Beach Motel on your right.
14. Go straight through the next traffic lights.
15. Go straight through the next roundabout.
16. Turn right at the next roundabout.
17. Turn left at the next roundabout. You will drive along the beachfront at Khor Fakkan, which has been grass and tree-lined.
18. Go straight through the next roundabout, which has the Oceanic Hotel on your right.
19. Go straight through the next roundabout.
20. Go straight through the next roundabout.
21. Go straight through the next roundabout.
22. Just after this roundabout is the turning on the left for the Wurrayah Waterfall but you are required to do a U-turn to get back to it.
23. Go straight through the next roundabout. The road changes from duel-carriageway to single. At the next headland you cross (52.1km) the view from the top is good. Shortly after this the road turns back to duel carriageway

100

CONTINUED ON PAGE 103

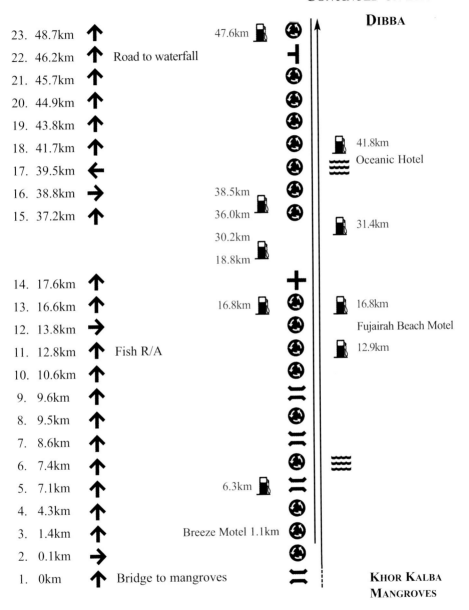

DIBBA

23. 48.7km ↑   47.6km

22. 46.2km ↑ Road to waterfall

21. 45.7km ↑

20. 44.9km ↑

19. 43.8km ↑

18. 41.7km ↑   41.8km
                        Oceanic Hotel

17. 39.5km ←

16. 38.8km →   38.5km

15. 37.2km ↑   36.0km   31.4km

                    30.2km

                    18.8km

14. 17.6km ↑

13. 16.6km ↑   16.8km   16.8km

12. 13.8km →   Fujairah Beach Motel

11. 12.8km ↑ Fish R/A   12.9km

10. 10.6km ↑

9. 9.6km ↑

8. 9.5km ↑

7. 8.6km ↑

6. 7.4km ↑

5. 7.1km ↑   6.3km

4. 4.3km ↑

3. 1.4km ↑ Breeze Motel 1.1km

2. 0.1km →

1. 0km ↑ Bridge to mangroves   KHOR KALBA
                                                    MANGROVES

24. Go straight past the next right turn. You can turn right here for Sandy Beach Motel and Snoopy Rock.
25. Go straight through the next roundabout
26. Turn left at the next roundabout. You can turn right here for Le Meridien Al Aqaa.
27. Go straight through the next roundabout (the big pot R/A)
28. At the next roundabout (the dolphin R/A), you can turn right into Dibba.
29. The next roundabout will have a big mosque across from you and the route ends here.

Khor Kalba to Dibba

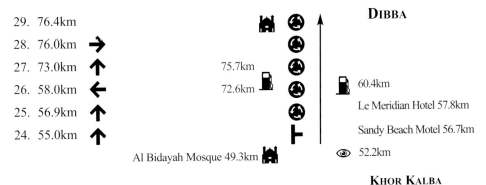

DIBBA

29. 76.4km
28. 76.0km
27. 73.0km
26. 58.0km
25. 56.9km
24. 55.0km

75.7km
72.6km

60.4km
Le Meridian Hotel 57.8km
Sandy Beach Motel 56.7km

52.2km

Al Bidayah Mosque 49.3km

KHOR KALBA MANGROVES

CONTINUED FROM PAGE 101

ROUTE KILOMETRES

STEP	ACTION	KM	DISTANCE KM	STEP	ACTION	KM	DISTANCE KM
			19.6	29.	End	76.4	
14.	Go straight	17.6					0.4
			1.0	28.	Turn right	76.0	
13.	Go straight	16.6					3.0
			2.8	27.	Go straight	73.0	
12.	Go straight	13.8					15.0
			1.0	26.	Turn left	58.0	
11.	Go straight	12.8					1.1
			2.2	25.	Go straight	56.9	
10.	Go straight	10.6					1.9
			1.0	24.	Go straight	55.0	
9.	Go straight	9.6					6.3
			0.1	23.	Go straight	48.7	
8.	Go straight	9.5					2.5
			0.9	22.	Go straight	46.2	
7.	Go straight	8.6					0.5
			1.2	21.	Go straight	45.7	
6.	Go straight	7.4					0.8
			0.3	20.	Go straight	44.9	
5.	Go straight	7.1					1.1
			2.8	19.	Go straight	43.8	
4.	Go straight	4.3					2.1
			2.9	18.	Go straight	41.7	
3.	Go straight	1.4					2.2
			1.3	17.	Turn left	39.5	
2.	Turn right	0.1					0.7
			0.1	16.	Turn right	38.8	
1.	Start	0.0					1.6
				15.	Go straight	37.2	

KHOR FAKKAN TO WADI WURAYYAH WATERFALL

ROAD QUALITY	✔✔✔✔
SHADE/AMENITIES	
ACCESSIBILITY	✔
TIME TAKEN	✔
MY RATING	✔✔

STARTING POINT:	Khor Fakkan Oceanic Hotel R/A
FINISHING POINT:	Wadi Wurayyah Waterfall
DISTANCE:	16.8km
ROAD CONDITIONS:	Very good tarred road all the way
THINGS TO SEE:	Waterfall, rugged mountains, gravel plains
NOTES:	The climb down the wadi to the waterfall is not easy

Wadi Wurayyah Waterfall is a stunning waterfall set in the Hajar Mountains. It is easy to get to on good tarred roads and the drive into the mountains is compelling with lots of photo opportunities as the road winds into the mountains crossing the deep Wurayyah Wadi. To actually get to the waterfall, you either need to climb down a steep track into the wadi or drive along the wadi in a 4x4 to the waterfall.

Unfortunately, due to the relatively easy access to this waterfall, it has been spoiled by inconsiderate people, who have left large amounts of smelly rubbish and graffiti on the rocks around the waterfall. This is a great pity as the waterfall and pool below it would be stunning in a pristine condition. Though the easy access makes it worth a visit, in many ways its beauty is better appreciated from afar at the top of the wadi.

Another possibility for the energetic and those not wanting to clamber down the loose gravel wadi walls, is to pull your car off the road at the third last wadi crossing and to hike along the wadi for 2.7km till you reach the pools and waterfall. Due to the wadi walls, you should get some shade. The extremely energetic can follow the stream above the waterfall and eventually reach a second pool and waterfall. This may not be the best option in summer.

Directions to Wadi Wurayyah Waterfall

1. At the roundabout near the entrance to the Oceanic Hotel, near Khor Fakkan Bay in Khor Fakkan, zero your odometer.
2. Drive towards Dibba going straight through the next roundabout.
3. Go straight through the next roundabout.
4. Go straight through the next roundabout.
5. Travel 1.1 km beyond the last roundabout, do a U-turn.
6. Drive back 700m and turn right. This road takes you away from the coast and into the mountains. After a few kilometers, to the left is a turning to a dam and water bottling plant. Continue straight on.
7. Wadi crossing.
8. Go straight past the turning for the bottling plant.
9. Take the right fork. The roads join up again shortly so either fork could be taken. You will cross Wadi Wurayyah in several spots.
10. Wadi crossing.
11. The road will merge with the road you would be on if you had taken the left fork previously.
12. Wadi crossing.
13. Wadi crossing. You can stop here and walk up the wadi to the waterfall 2.7km or drive along the wadi but some of the rocks are big so is best only done in a 4 wheel drive.
14. Wadi crossing.
15. Wadi crossing.
16. Eventually the road will come to an end. From here at the top of the wadi you have a good view of the pools and waterfall. You can clamber down the side of the wadi on a steep loose rock track to the pools and waterfall.

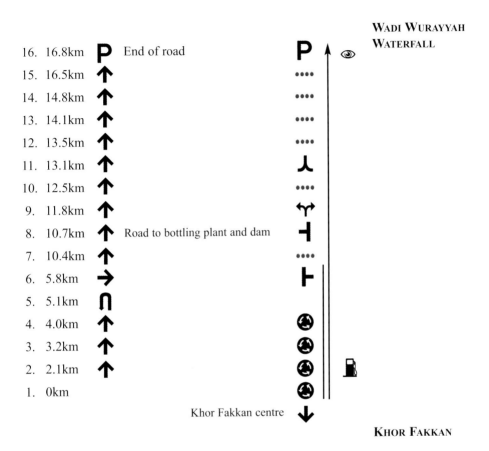

16. 16.8km   P   End of road

15. 16.5km

14. 14.8km

13. 14.1km

12. 13.5km

11. 13.1km

10. 12.5km

9. 11.8km

8. 10.7km   Road to bottling plant and dam

7. 10.4km

6. 5.8km

5. 5.1km

4. 4.0km

3. 3.2km

2. 2.1km

1. 0km

Khor Fakkan centre

WADI WURAYYAH WATERFALL

KHOR FAKKAN

107

ROUTE KILOMETRES

STEP	ACTION	KM	DISTANCE KM	STEP	ACTION	KM	DISTANCE KM
8.	Go straight	10.7		16.	End	16.8	
			0.3				0.3
7.	Go straight	10.4		15.	Go straight	16.5	
			9.6				1.7
6.	Turn right	5.8		14.	Go straight	14.8	
			0.7				0.7
5.	U turn	5.1		13.	Go straight	14.1	
			1.1				0.6
4.	Go straight	4.0		12.	Go straight	13.5	
			0.8				0.4
3.	Go straight	3.2		11.	Go straight	13.1	
			1.1				0.6
2.	Go straight	2.1		10.	Go straight	12.5	
			2.1				0.7
1.	Start	0		9.	Take right fork	11.8	
							10.1

DIBBA TO AL DHAID

ROAD QUALITY	✓✓✓✓✓
SHADE/AMENITIES	✓✓✓
ACCESSIBILITY	✓✓✓✓✓
TIME TAKEN	✓✓✓
MY RATING	✓✓✓✓

STARTING POINT:	Dibba dolphin R/A
FINISHING POINT:	Al Dhaid
DISTANCE:	70.2km
ROAD CONDITIONS:	Very good tarred road all the way
THINGS TO SEE:	Stunning planted gorge, Friday Market, mountains and deep wadis
NOTES:	Be prepared to bargain if you want a good deal at the market.

This route appears to be your average drive through the mountains in the UAE. The mountains as well as the deep wadi running along the road are impressive, but one needs to stop to catch the stunning picture opportunities along this route. At one point, the road crosses a deep wadi that has been carved into the rock. This has been used to plant mangoes and dates and they seem to be growing well, shaded by the walls of the wadi and watered by the occasional water flowing down it. From the road you get a great vantage point looking down and along this wadi on both sides of the road. About 100 metres before this, there is another wadi that is also planted. Dramatic awe-inspiring gorges and wadis carved into the rock are a feature on the majority of the route.

Other places to stop are the market stalls before and after Masafi. The (inaptly named) Friday Market after Masafi is open every day and has loads of carpet stalls, clay pots stalls a number of plant and fruit and vegetable stalls. The stalls before Masafi are a bit quirky and provide a different range of items from the mass of manufactured carpets sold elsewhere.

DIRECTIONS TO AL DHAID

1. Starting at the Dolphin Roundabout take the road signposted to Masafi on the **E89**.
2. Go straight through the roundabout.
3. Go straight past the turning for Fujairah Cement Industries.
4. Go straight through the roundabout.
5. Go straight past the turning for Dibba Mineral Water Plant.
6. Go straight past the turning for Al Hala. At 20.6km, 20.8km and 21km there are deep wadi gorges planted with date palms and other trees. These provide for great photo opportunities. Just pull up on the hard shoulder.
7. Go straight across the bridge.
8. Go straight past the turning for Tayyabah.
9. Go straight past the turning for Masafi Town. Just past the turning on both sides of the road at 35.1km there are a few market stalls.
10. At the Masafi roundabout turn right onto the **E89** signposted to Sharjah. This is the end of the Dubai to Masafi route page 148. It is also the beginning of the Masafi to Fujairah route page 77.
11. Go straight past the turning for Marbad.
12. You cross a bridge.
13. You cross another bridge. At 44km is the Friday market on both sides of the road.
14. You cross another bridge.
15. Go straight past the turning for Ras Al Khaimah **E18**.
16. At the next roundabout, go straight. Turning right would take you to Ras Al Khaimah.
17. At the next roundabout Mosque Square, with the big mosque turn left.
18. At the next roundabout, Hisn Square the route ends you can go straight on the **E55** for Hatta and Al Ain or turn right on the **E88** to Sharjah and Dubai.

Dibba to Al Dhaid

AL DHAID

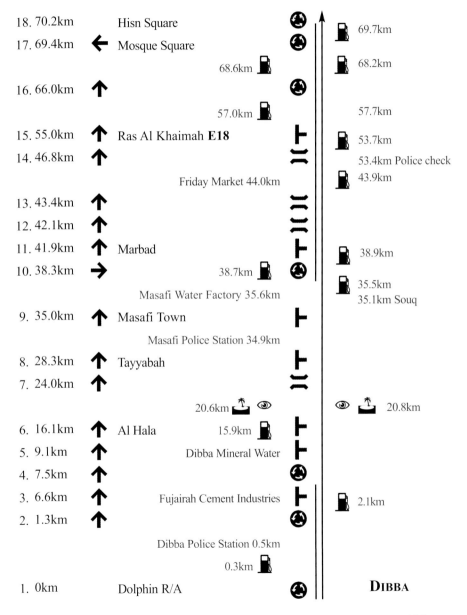

18. 70.2km   Hisn Square   69.7km

17. 69.4km ← Mosque Square

68.6km   68.2km

16. 66.0km ↑

57.0km   57.7km

15. 55.0km ↑ Ras Al Khaimah **E18**   53.7km

14. 46.8km ↑   53.4km Police check

Friday Market 44.0km   43.9km

13. 43.4km ↑

12. 42.1km ↑

11. 41.9km ↑ Marbad   38.9km

10. 38.3km →   38.7km

35.5km

Masafi Water Factory 35.6km   35.1km Souq

9. 35.0km ↑ Masafi Town

Masafi Police Station 34.9km

8. 28.3km ↑ Tayyabah

7. 24.0km ↑

20.6km / 20.8km

6. 16.1km ↑ Al Hala   15.9km

5. 9.1km ↑ Dibba Mineral Water

4. 7.5km ↑

3. 6.6km ↑ Fujairah Cement Industries   2.1km

2. 1.3km ↑

Dibba Police Station 0.5km

0.3km

1. 0km   Dolphin R/A   **DIBBA**

ROUTE KILOMETRES

STEP	ACTION	KM	DISTANCE KM	STEP	ACTION	KM	DISTANCE KM
9.	Go straight	35.0		18.	End	70.2	
			6.7				0.8
8.	Go straight	28.3		17.	Go straight	69.4	
			4.3				3.4
7.	Go straight	24.0		16.	Go straight	66.0	
			7.9				11.0
6.	Go straight	16.1		15.	Go straight	55.0	
			7.0				8.2
5.	Go straight	9.1		14.	Go straight	46.8	
			1.6				3.4
4.	Go straight	7.5		13.	Go straight	43.4	
			0.9				1.3
3.	Go straight	6.6		12.	Go straight	42.1	
			5.3				0.2
2.	Go straight	1.3		11.	Go straight	41.9	
			1.3				3.6
1.	Start	0		10.	Turn right	38.3	
							3.3

THE DATE PALM

The exact origin of the date palm is not known, but evidence of date palm cultivation goes as far back as 4000 B.C. in what is now southern Iraq. References to date palms have also been found in ancient Egypt and it seems that the earliest form of date palm cultivation coincided with the oldest civilizations and originated in North-East Africa, stretching east into the delta of the Euphrates, Tigris and Indus Valley. Had the date palm not existed, it is unlikely hot and barren parts of the world like the UAE would not have been populated and developed. However even the date palm is not able to survive in the desert without a good source of water and the traveller will note many palms that used to grow along dry wadis which now seem to be dying as increased demand has been put on the ground water reducing that available to the date palms. The number of wild date palms outside the oasis has, therefore, decreased. However, the UAE has been actively planting date palms along the sides of major roads and creating new date plantations, which survive as a result of regular watering. Thus, annual date production in the UAE has jumped from less than 8,000 metric tonnes in 1971 to more than 500,000 metric tonnes in 2000. It is said that "the date palm likes its feet in Heaven and its head in Hell", because the date palm needs a good water supply and high temperatures. As long as the date palm has this good water supply, it seems not to be affected by temperatures of 50°C and higher, which is fortunate because the temperatures in the UAE in summer often soar. The date palm is protected from the heat because it only has one growing point, on top of the trunk well encased in the bases of older fronds made of highly insulating material. By the time the new fronds and fruit and flower bunches sprouting from this growing point have to face the sun, they are already tough enough to withstand the heat. In spite of this insulation, the growing point would eventually heat up if the date palm did not have a cooling effect from water slowly rising in the trunk and evaporating through the leaves. Walking into an oasis you will notice the temperature can drop by as much as 5°C. Date palms will flower only when the shade temperature rises over 18°C and will fruit at temperatures above 25°C, while vegetative growth will stop under 10°C. It is the female date palm that produces the dates thus the oasis is comprised mainly of female date palms with males only needed for fertilization. Harvesting of date palms in the UAE takes place between late

115

June and early October the hottest months of the year. During the first week of August, there is an annual date festival at Liwa, where date growers present their various products.

Before the UAE relied on its oil wealth, dates were vital for survival. The date palm provided a concentrated energy food 3000 calories/kg; it also provided shade and protection from the desert winds. Tamr, made from boiling and compressing dates could be kept for long periods of time due to the preservative qualities of the high sugar content. The dried palm fronds could be plaited into containers for the tamr and dried dates providing a major source of food in the desert, for mariners at sea, armies and caravan travellers. Any left over could be used to feed domestic animals. The dates could also be stacked into storerooms designed with underlying drainage to collect the prized date syrup. The date palm was used for more than a source of food. Practically all parts of the palm could be utilised. Due to the lack of timber in the UAE date palm fronds were used instead of wood for the walls and roofs of houses. The palm trunk could be formed into a mortar for crushing wheat with the tree stump shaped into a pestle. Palm tree trunks also supported the roofs of mud brick and stone castles and towers and small boats could be

made from the midrib of the palm frond.

Dates are still a popular food in the UAE, especially to break the fast during Ramadan. Dates are now turned into luxury treats stuffed with almonds or covered in chocolate. It is amazing to go into a date shop in the UAE and see how this fruit can be transformed into a variety of sweets. Palm fronds are still woven into baskets, bags, bowls, food covers, floor mats and made into sweeping brushes. Boats with palm tree spines can still be seen on the East Coast. There are more than 50 varieties of date palm in the UAE, but prosperity has reduced the UAE's dependence on dates. However, with the aid of modern technology and intensive planting, date-palm cultivation has been transformed into a major agricultural industry serving export and domestic markets. Today, there are over 40 million date palms planted in the UAE.

117

ABU DHABI TO LIWA OASIS

ROAD QUALITY	✔✔✔✔✔
SHADE/AMENITIES	✔✔✔
ACCESSIBILITY	✔✔✔✔✔
TIME TAKEN	✔✔✔✔✔
MY RATING	✔✔✔✔

STARTING POINT:	Where E22 joins E11
FINISHING POINT:	Mezaira'a
DISTANCE:	195.7km
ROAD CONDITIONS:	Very good dual-carriage way all the way
THINGS TO SEE:	Stunning dunes and oasis, forts.
NOTES:	Petrol stations with good facilities.

The route from Abu Dhabi to Liwa Oasis is an extremely diverse one, showing much of the UAE's past and present. The oasis reflects the accomplishments of the past, Arabia's supreme achievement of turning the desert green, while the oil fields on the way reflect the wealth of the present and the UAE's transformation into an industrialised society. The road outside Abu Dhabi is heavily planted with date palms and salt-resistant trees, but this quickly gives way to vast expanses of salt plains with a few scrubs and low bushes. The UAE government is in the process of establishing date plantations along the route, but these are as yet small and scraggly, fighting against the wind, salt and sand. As you near Madinat Zayed, the landscape changes into one of high white dunes. This is a pristine landscape with none of the ubiquitous litter of many routes, only clean, dramatic sculptures of sand. Soon the white sand becomes shot with red and grey, creating a kaleidoscope in sand. As you near the town of Madinat Zayed, you will start to see forests and date plantations. After the town, more forests compete with dunes and, if you are lucky, you will see small gazelles in the Hezam Al Zayed Forestry area. A drive down the dirt road at Al Kabshiya Forest is a pleasant detour although most of the forests are fenced off from the public. Finally, you will reach Mezaira'a, the first village of Liwa Oasis. Liwa Oasis is not one central oasis, but rather consists of a series of villages or hamlets, each with their own oasis.

From the Mezaira'a roundabout you can turn right to Arrada or left to Hameem. If you turn right to Arrada, the route, which I call 'The Valley of the

Dunes', has particularly impressive dunes encompassing the vivid green of plantations of palm and other trees and three forts. The first is just after the next roundabout underneath the green hillside of the palace. You might not be able to see it from the road as it is behind the date palms and you will need to turn down a dirt road to get to it. Further down the road is a small fort on the side of the road outside Dhafeer and a larger fort just before Qotouf. Its turret can be seen from the road rising above the date palms and you can take a dirt road down to it. These forts provide impressive photo opportunities. The road culminates at Arrada where the tarred road gives way to dirt, which is currently being tarred. If you followed this dirt road, it would eventually take you all the way to the Saudi Arabian border!

If you turn left towards Hameem at the Mezaira'a roundabout, the oases of Shah and Tharwaniyah are particularly impressive. There are numerous opportunities to turn off the road and explore the oases on the way. One interesting fort is the one at Attab that you will find on your way back towards Mezaira'a if you turn at the sign for Attab and then into the car park, you will see a charming little fort. This fort provides excellent photo opportunities with dunes and plantations in the distance.

DIRECTIONS TO LIWA OASIS

1. The route starts on the **E11** where the **E22** joins the **E11** heading away from Dubai to Sila.
2. You will cross a bridge going over the truck road at 4.8km. At 53.2km you will go through a police checkpoint.
3. You will cross another bridge.
4. At 82.7 km take the turning to Madinat Zayed and Mezaira'a.
5. At the roundabout at the end of the feed road, turn left
6. Go over a bridge crossing the **E11**.
7. At the next roundabout go straight.
8. At 92.4 km you will cross a bridge over a pipeline this road to Liwa will cross a number of bridges like this and ones crossing side roads. I have not marked them all.
9.-15. You will go straight through 7 sets of traffic lights as you drive through Madinat Zayed.
16. At 192.8 kilometres, as you enter Mezaira'a, you will go straight through a roundabout.
17. At 195.7 kilometres you will reach a roundabout, which is the end of the route. You can turn right here for the Liwa Hotel and Rest House and the drive to Arrada or you can turn left for the drive to Hameen.

ROUTE KILOMETRES

STEP	ACTION	KM	DISTANCE KM	STEP	ACTION	KM	DISTANCE KM
9.	Go straight	133.0		17.	End	195.7	
			40.6				1.9
8.	Go straight	92.4		16.	Go straight	193.8	
			7.2				56.0
7.	Go straight	85.2		15.	Go straight	137.8	
			0.8				0.7
6.	Go straight	84.4		14.	Go straight	137.1	
			1.0				0.8
5.	Turn left	83.4		13.	Go straight	136.3	
			0.7				0.5
4.	Turn right	82.7		12.	Go straight	135.8	
			6.1				0.4
3.	Go straight	76.6		11.	Go straight	135.4	
			71.8				1.0
2.	Go straight	4.8		10.	Go straight	134.4	
			4.8				1.4
1.	Start	0					

MEZAIRA'A

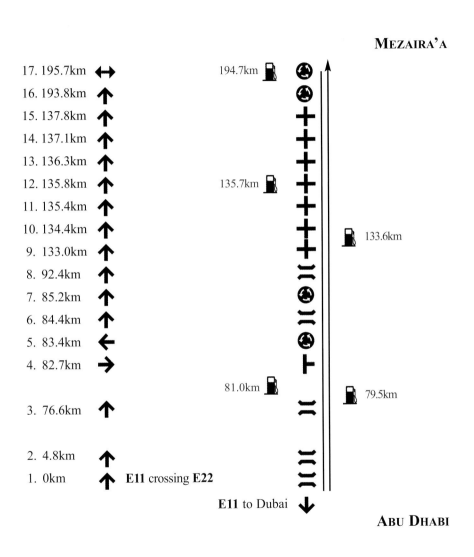

17. 195.7km ↔　　　194.7km 🚰

16. 193.8km ↑

15. 137.8km ↑

14. 137.1km ↑

13. 136.3km ↑

12. 135.8km ↑　　　135.7km 🚰

11. 135.4km ↑

10. 134.4km ↑　　　　　　　　　　🚰 133.6km

9. 133.0km ↑

8. 92.4km ↑

7. 85.2km ↑

6. 84.4km ↑

5. 83.4km ←

4. 82.7km →

　　　　　　　81.0km 🚰　　　🚰 79.5km

3. 76.6km ↑

2. 4.8km ↑

1. 0km ↑ **E11** crossing **E22**

E11 to Dubai ↓

ABU DHABI

123

FEEDER ROUTES

The feeder routes have been created to provide a route for people travelling from Abu Dhabi or Dubai to the start of most of the routes included in *On-Road in the UAE*. The routes point out places of interest along the way to the starting points as well as roads that can be taken to get to other parts of the UAE. Not all turnings have been included and most farm access roads and U-turns have not been shown.

ABU DHABI TO AL AIN (E22)

The route from Abu Dhabi to Al Ain on the **E22** is a fast road surrounded in parts by big impressive sand dunes. The only obstacles one encounters are the numerous roundabouts in Al Ain.

1. The route starts on the Maqta Bridge.
2. Go straight. You can take the feed road here which will join the **E10** and then the **E11** for Dubai
3. Go straight. Turning for Musaffah.
4. Go straight. You can take the feed road to get to the **E11** for Dubai, the **E33**, also joins the **E66**, a possible way to get to Hatta and the East Coast from Abu Dhabi.
5. Go straight. The off ramp here is for Emirates Road which you can take to the airport or in the other direction to Jebel Ali and on to Abu Dhabi on the **E11**
6. Go straight past turning for Mahawi.
7. Go straight past turning for Musaffah.
8. Go straight past turning for Liwa on the **E11** this is where the route to Liwa on page 119 starts.
9. Go straight past turning for the **E11** to Dubai.
10. Go straight past turning for Baniyas West.
11. Go straight past turning for Baniyas East.
12. Go straight past turning for Al Wathba South.
13. Go straight past turning for Al Wathba Truck Road.
14. Go straight past turning for Al Wathba South.
15. Go straight past turning for Al Nahda and the camel race track.
16. Go straight past turning for Zayed Military City.
17. Go straight past turning for Al Khatim South and Boudthib Endurance Village
18. Go straight past turning for Al Khatim Truck Road.
19. Go straight past turning for Police station / Civil Defence Centre.
20. Go straight past turning for Al Khazna Palace.
21. Go straight past turning for Al Khazna South.
22. Go straight past turning for Al Khazna.
23. Go straight past turning for Police Station.
24. Go straight past turning for Remah Truck Road.

126

AL AIN

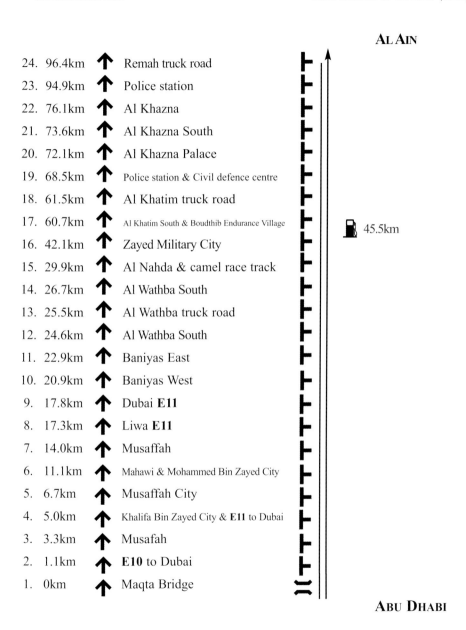

24.	96.4km ⬆	Remah truck road
23.	94.9km ⬆	Police station
22.	76.1km ⬆	Al Khazna
21.	73.6km ⬆	Al Khazna South
20.	72.1km ⬆	Al Khazna Palace
19.	68.5km ⬆	Police station & Civil defence centre
18.	61.5km ⬆	Al Khatim truck road
17.	60.7km ⬆	Al Khatim South & Boudthib Endurance Village
16.	42.1km ⬆	Zayed Military City
15.	29.9km ⬆	Al Nahda & camel race track
14.	26.7km ⬆	Al Wathba South
13.	25.5km ⬆	Al Wathba truck road
12.	24.6km ⬆	Al Wathba South
11.	22.9km ⬆	Baniyas East
10.	20.9km ⬆	Baniyas West
9.	17.8km ⬆	Dubai **E11**
8.	17.3km ⬆	Liwa **E11**
7.	14.0km ⬆	Musaffah
6.	11.1km ⬆	Mahawi & Mohammed Bin Zayed City
5.	6.7km ⬆	Musaffah City
4.	5.0km ⬆	Khalifa Bin Zayed City & **E11** to Dubai
3.	3.3km ⬆	Musafah
2.	1.1km ⬆	**E10** to Dubai
1.	0km ⬆	Maqta Bridge

⛽ 45.5km

ABU DHABI

25. Go straight past turning for Police Station.
26. Go straight past turning for Abu Samra.
27. Go straight past turning for Al Saad and the road to Sweihan from here you can head for Al Haiyir and the **E66**.
28. Go straight past turning for Al Saad the date factory is also on the other side of the road.
29. Go straight past turning for Al Yahar.
30. Go straight past turning for Al Yahar.
31. Go straight past turning for Al Salamat and Al Ain Airport.
32. Go straight past turning for Military school.
33. Go straight past turning for Al Bateen.
34. Go straight, crossing a bridge.
35. Go straight past turning for Shabiyat Al Magham.
36. Go straight through the traffic lights.
37. Go straight past turning for the equestrian centre.
38. Go straight across the Twam Roundabout following the signs to Town Centre.
39. Go straight across the next roundabout.
40. Go straight past feed road for Al Jimi.
41. Go straight under the underpass.
42. Go straight past feed road for Al Jimi.
43. Go straight under the underpass.
44. Go straight through the Sheikh Zayed Roundabout. To get to the Muwajii Fort you would go right round the roundabout returning back on yourself. Do not go under the underpass but take the feed road off to the right and the entrance to the fort is on your right.
45. Go straight across the next roundabout.
46. Go straight across the next roundabout (Planning Roundabout).
47. Turn right at the next roundabout.
48. You have now reached the Shekha Salama Mosque Roundabout. This is the starting point for the route to Jabel Hafeet page 19, the route to Khadra page 25, the route to Khutwa page 33, the route to Al Qua'a page 47, the route to Bida bint Saud page 53 and the route Al Ain to Hatta through Oman page 59.

AL AIN

48. 147.8km ↑ Sheikha Salama Mosque R/A

47. 147.5km →

46. 146.8km ↑ Planning R/A

45. 146.0km ↑

44. 145.4km ↑ Sheikh Zayed R/A

43. 144.5km ↑ Muwajii Fort 145km

42. 143.9km ↑ Al Jimi

41. 142.9km ↑

40. 142.3km ↑ Al Jimi

39. 139.0km ↑   139.5km

38. 135.3km ↑ Twam R/A

37. 134.1km ↑ Equestrian centre

36. 133.4km ↑

35. 129.7km ↑ Shabiyat Al Magham

34. 129.2km ↑

33. 128.3km ↑ Al Bateen

32. 128.0km ↑ Truck road & military school

31. 125.1km ↑ Al Salamat & airport

30. 121.2km ↑ Al Yahar

29. 116.9km ↑ Al Yahar Aailah compound

28. 116.1km ↑ Al Saad Industrial Area & Date factory

27. 110.7km ↑ Al Saad/Sweiham **E66**   106.2km Lay-by Mosque

26. 102.8km ↑ Abu Samra

25. 99.4km ↑ Remah South

ABU DHABI

129

ROUTE KILOMETRES

Step	Action	KM	Distance km	Step	Action	KM	Distance km
24.	Go straight	96.4		48.	End	147.8	
			1.5				0.3
23.	Go straight	94.9		47.	Turn right	147.5	
			18.8				0.7
22.	Go straight	76.1		46.	Go straight	146.8	
			2.5				0.8
21.	Go straight	73.6		45.	Go straight	146.0	
			1.5				0.6
20.	Go straight	72.1		44.	Go straight	145.4	
			3.6				0.9
19.	Go straight	68.5		43.	Go straight	144.5	
			7.0				0.6
18.	Go straight	61.5		42.	Go straight	143.9	
			0.8				1.0
17.	Go straight	60.7		41.	Go straight	142.9	
			18.6				0.6
16.	Go straight	42.1		40.	Go straight	142.3	
			12.2				3.3
15.	Go straight	29.9		39.	Go straight	139.0	
			3.2				3.7
14.	Go straight	26.7		38.	Go straight	135.3	
			1.7				1.2
13.	Go straight	25.5		37.	Go straight	134.1	
			0.9				0.7
12.	Go straight	24.6		36.	Go straight	133.4	
			1.7				3.7
11.	Go straight	22.9		35.	Go straight	129.7	
			2.0				0.5
10.	Go straight	20.9		34.	Go straight	129.2	
			3.1				0.9
9.	Go straight	17.8		33.	Go straight	128.3	
			0.5				0.3
8.	Go straight	17.3		32.	Go straight	128.0	
			3.3				2.9
7.	Go straight	14.0		31.	Go straight	125.1	
			2.9				3.9
6.	Go straight	11.1		30.	Go straight	121.2	
			4.4				4.3
5.	Go straight	6.7		29.	Go straight	116.9	
			1.7				0.8
4.	Go straight	5.0		28.	Go straight	116.1	
			1.7				5.4
3.	Go straight	3.3		27.	Go straight	110.7	
			0.2				7.9
2.	Go straight	1.1		26.	Go straight	102.8	
			1.1				3.4
1.	Start	0		25.	Go straight	99.4	
							3.0

ABU DHABI TO DUBAI (E11)

I have included this run along the coast on the **E10** then **E11** to allow people coming from Abu Dhabi to link up with routes on the East Coast and Hatta, though some may find it more interesting to use the **E33** or cut the corner off using the **E77**. At the time of writing, there was a lot of construction as you come into Dubai this may lead to a number of new interchanges.

1. The route starts on the Maqta Bridge.
2. Take the feed road here to get on the **E10** to Dubai. Going straight would put you on the **E22** to Al Ain.
3. Go straight across the overpass.
4. Go straight past turning for Al Raha Beach.
5. Go straight past turning for Khalifa City and Golf Club.
6. Go straight past the turning for Khalifa City, Al Raha Beach & Abu Dhabi International Airport.
7. Go straight over the bridge.
8. Go straight past turning for Mafraq.
9. Go straight past turning for Zayed Military City.
10. Go straight past turning for Al Rahba City.
11. Go straight past turning for Al Rahba City.
12. Go straight past turning for Al Samha East and West.
13. Go straight past turning for Al Semeih and the camel race track.
14. Go straight past turning for Saih As Sidirah.
15. Go straight past turning for the camel racetrack.
16. Go straight past turning for Ghantoot and the Jazira Resort Polo Club.
17. Go straight. You can take this off ramp to get to the **E311**; which cross the **E66** to Al Ain and the **E44** to Hatta. The **E311** can also be used to bypass Dubai for Dubai airport.
18. Go straight past turning for Jebel Ali Hotel and the **E311**.
19. Go straight past turning for Dubai Investment Park and for a link to Al Ain and Hatta.
20. Go straight. You can take this off ramp to get to the **E311**, which crosses the **E66** to Al Ain and the **E44** to Hatta and the **E77**; which joins the **E66** to Al Ain.
21. Go straight past turning for The Gardens, Jebel Ali Village and the **E59**.
22. Go straight past the turning for The Gardens and Jumeirah Island.
23. Go straight past turning for Al Sufah and the Dubai Marina.

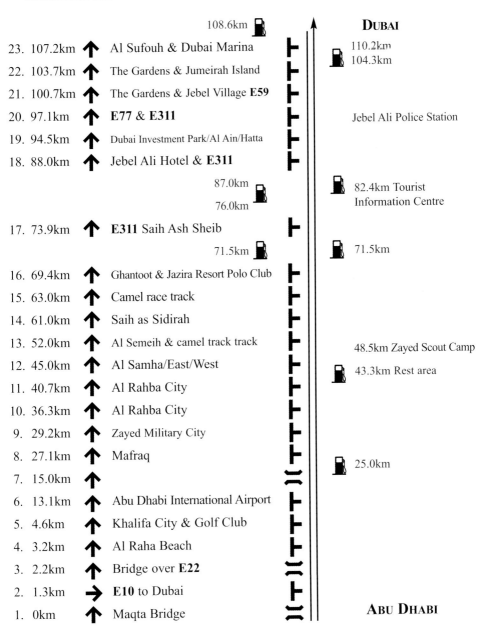

		108.6km 🛢	**DUBAI**
23.	107.2km ⬆	Al Sufouh & Dubai Marina	110.2km
			104.3km
22.	103.7km ⬆	The Gardens & Jumeirah Island	
21.	100.7km ⬆	The Gardens & Jebel Village **E59**	
20.	97.1km ⬆	**E77 & E311**	Jebel Ali Police Station
19.	94.5km ⬆	Dubai Investment Park/Al Ain/Hatta	
18.	88.0km ⬆	Jebel Ali Hotel & **E311**	
		87.0km 🛢	82.4km Tourist
		76.0km	Information Centre
17.	73.9km ⬆	**E311** Saih Ash Sheib	
		71.5km 🛢	71.5km
16.	69.4km ⬆	Ghantoot & Jazira Resort Polo Club	
15.	63.0km ⬆	Camel race track	
14.	61.0km ⬆	Saih as Sidirah	
13.	52.0km ⬆	Al Semeih & camel track track	48.5km Zayed Scout Camp
12.	45.0km ⬆	Al Samha/East/West	43.3km Rest area
11.	40.7km ⬆	Al Rahba City	
10.	36.3km ⬆	Al Rahba City	
9.	29.2km ⬆	Zayed Military City	
8.	27.1km ⬆	Mafraq	25.0km
7.	15.0km ⬆		
6.	13.1km ⬆	Abu Dhabi International Airport	
5.	4.6km ⬆	Khalifa City & Golf Club	
4.	3.2km ⬆	Al Raha Beach	
3.	2.2km ⬆	Bridge over **E22**	
2.	1.3km ➡	**E10** to Dubai	
1.	0km ⬆	Maqta Bridge	**ABU DHABI**

24. Go straight past turning for Al Barsha.
25. Go straight past turning for Umm Suqeim / Al Quoz Industrial Area
26. Go straight past turning for Al Safa Park and camel & horse racing track.
27. Go straight. You can take the off ramp here to join up with the **E44** to Hatta.
28. Go straight past turning for World Trade Centre Exhibition Halls.
29. Go straight past turning for Bar Dubai Za'abeel.
30. Go straight under the underpass.
31. Bear right. You can bear left for Bur Dubai.
32. Go straight. Turn here for the start of the feeder routes to Al Ain, Masafi and Hatta.
33. Go straight Under the Underpass.
34. Go straight. The flyover above is the start of the feeder route to Al Ain, Masafi and Hatta.
35. Go straight. Wafi City is on your left. You can carry on along the **E11** into Dubai and on to Sharjah.

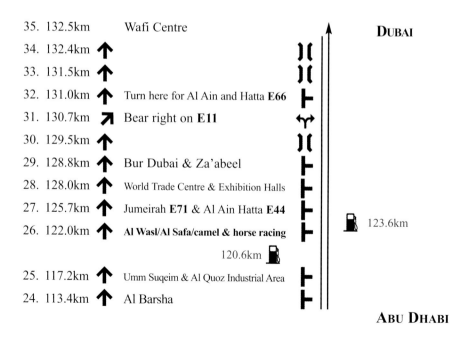

35. 132.5km   Wafi Centre   **DUBAI**
34. 132.4km
33. 131.5km
32. 131.0km   Turn here for Al Ain and Hatta **E66**
31. 130.7km   Bear right on **E11**
30. 129.5km
29. 128.8km   Bur Dubai & Za'abeel
28. 128.0km   World Trade Centre & Exhibition Halls
27. 125.7km   Jumeirah **E71** & Al Ain Hatta **E44**
26. 122.0km   **Al Wasl/Al Safa/camel & horse racing**
                              123.6km
                 120.6km
25. 117.2km   Umm Suqeim & Al Quoz Industrial Area
24. 113.4km   Al Barsha
                                                        ABU DHABI

134

Route Kilometres

Step	Action	KM	Distance km	Step	Action	KM	Distance km
18.	Go straight	88.0		35.	Wafi City	132.5	
			14.1				0.1
17.	Go straight	73.9		34.	End	132.4	
			4.5				0.9
16.	Go straight	69.4		33.	Go straight	131.5	
			6.4				0.5
15.	Go straight	63.0		32.	Go straight	131.0	
			2.0				0.3
14.	Go straight	61.0		31.	Bear right	130.7	
			9.0				1.2
13.	Go straight	52.0		30.	Go straight	129.5	
			7.0				0.7
12.	Go straight	45.0		29.	Go straight	128.8	
			4.3				0.8
11.	Go straight	40.7		28.	Go straight	128.0	
			4.4				2.3
10.	Go straight	36.3		27.	Go straight	125.7	
			7.1				3.7
9.	Go straight	29.2		26.	Go straight	122.0	
			2.1				4.8
8.	Go straight	27.1		25.	Go straight	117.2	
			12.1				3.8
7.	Go straight	15.0		24.	Go straight	113.4	
			1.9				6.2
6.	Go straight	13.1		23.	Go straight	107.2	
			8.5				3.5
5.	Go straight	4.6		22.	Go straight	103.7	
			1.4				3.0
4.	Go straight	3.2		21.	Go straight	100.7	
			1.0				3.6
3.	Go straight	2.2		20.	Go straight	97.1	
			0.9				2.6
2.	Turn right	1.3		19.	Go straight	94.5	
			1.3				6.5
1.	Start	0					

DUBAI TO AL AIN (E66)

The Dubai Al Ain road **E66** is a fast straight road where the only obstacles you encounter are two roundabouts leaving Dubai, and when you reach Al Ain, its numerous roundabouts. There are a number of turnings off the road to enable you to U- turn back to Dubai, but I have not included them in the route details.

1. The route starts where the **E66** (Oud Metha Road) crosses over the **E11** opposite Wafi City.
2. Go straight through the roundabout (1st exit) and continue along Oud Metha Road. On your left hand side at the end of Dubai Creek a large number of flamingos can be seen in the Dubai Wildlife and Waterbird Sanctuary.
3. Go straight through the Bin Khidra Exchange.
4. Go straight past the turning for Nad Al Sheba.
5. Go straight. The off ramp here is for Emirates Road (**E311**) which you can take to the airport or in the other direction to Jebel Ali and on to Abu Dhabi on the **E11**
6. Go straight.
7. Go straight. The off ramp here is for the **E611** which you can take to get to the start of the Khor Kalba Mangroves route page 93.
8. Go straight past the turning for Umm Nahad.
9. Go straight. You can take this off ramp for the **E77** for Abu Dhabi.
10. Go straight. You can take this off ramp for the **E77**, which will join up to the **E44** to Hatta.
11. Go straight past turning for Seih Assalem Endurance Village.
12. Go straight past turning for Margham
13. Go straight past turning for Murquab
14. Go straight past turning for Al Faqa
15. Go straight past turning for Al Faqa
16. Go straight past turning. You can take this off ramp to get to Fujairah, Al Dhaid, Hatta and Shwaib on the **E55**
17. Go straight past turning for the **E33** to Abu Dhabi.
18. Go straight through the roundabout, the road becomes Emirates Street.
19. Go straight through the roundabout.
20. Go straight through the roundabout. You can turn left here for Hili Archaeological Park.
21. Turn left. Turning right here takes you to Bida bint Saud page 53.
22. Continue straight through the roundabout on Mohammad Ibn Khalifa Street.
23. Go straight through the Al Rumailah roundabout. You can turn left here for Hili Oasis.

136

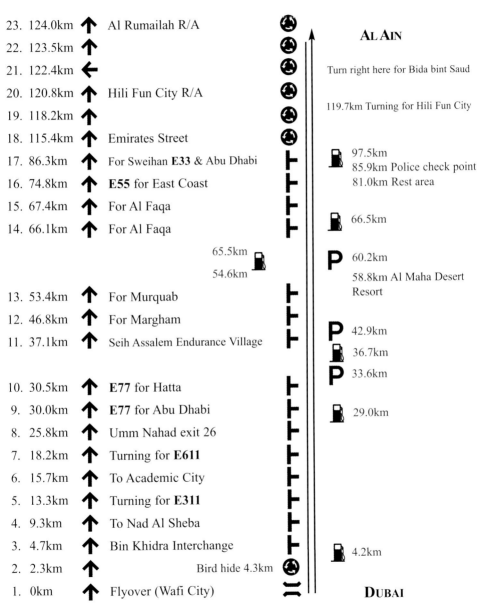

23. 124.0km ↑ Al Rumailah R/A
22. 123.5km ↑
21. 122.4km ←
20. 120.8km ↑ Hili Fun City R/A
19. 118.2km ↑
18. 115.4km ↑ Emirates Street
17. 86.3km ↑ For Sweihan **E33** & Abu Dhabi
16. 74.8km ↑ **E55** for East Coast
15. 67.4km ↑ For Al Faqa
14. 66.1km ↑ For Al Faqa

65.5km
54.6km

13. 53.4km ↑ For Murquab
12. 46.8km ↑ For Margham
11. 37.1km ↑ Seih Assalem Endurance Village

10. 30.5km ↑ **E77** for Hatta
9. 30.0km ↑ **E77** for Abu Dhabi
8. 25.8km ↑ Umm Nahad exit 26
7. 18.2km ↑ Turning for **E611**
6. 15.7km ↑ To Academic City
5. 13.3km ↑ Turning for **E311**
4. 9.3km ↑ To Nad Al Sheba
3. 4.7km ↑ Bin Khidra Interchange
2. 2.3km ↑ Bird hide 4.3km
1. 0km ↑ Flyover (Wafi City)

AL AIN

Turn right here for Bida bint Saud

119.7km Turning for Hili Fun City

97.5km
85.9km Police check point
81.0km Rest area

66.5km

60.2km
58.8km Al Maha Desert Resort

42.9km
36.7km
33.6km

29.0km

4.2km

DUBAI

137

24. Go straight through the roundabout. You can turn left here for Hili Archaeological Park.
25. Go straight through the next roundabout
26. Go straight. You can turn right here for Al Qattara Oasis and Al Jimi Oasis
27. Go straight through the Al Khrais roundabout.
28. Go straight at the roundabout.
29. Go straight across the bridge.
30. Turn left at the Zayed Central Library Roundabout onto Shakhboot Ibn Sultan Street. You can go straight along this road to get to the turning for Buraimi.
31. Take the feed road right at the traffic lights onto Al Ain Street.
32. Turn left at the Al Mandoos (Jewellery Box) Roundabout onto Ali Ibn Abi Taleb Street.
33. Turn right at Globe Roundabout onto Salahuddeen Al Ayyubi Street.
34. Go straight on at the next roundabout on Salahuddeen Al Ayyubi Street.
35. You have now reached the Sheika Salama Mosque roundabout in the centre of Al Ain at 132.5km. This is the starting point for the route to Jebel Hafeet page 19, the route to Khadra page 25, the route to Khutwa page 33 the route to Al Qua'a page 47, the route to Bida bint Saud page 53 and the route Al Ain to Hatta through Oman page 59.

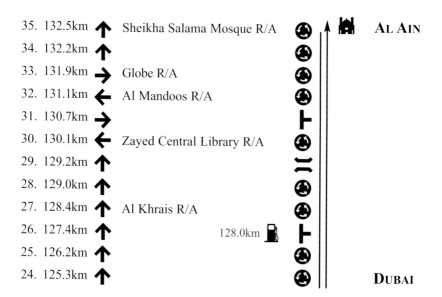

ROUTE KILOMETRES

STEP	ACTION	KM	DISTANCE KM	STEP	ACTION	KM	DISTANCE KM
18.	Go straight	115.4		35.	End	132.5	
			29.1				0.3
17.	Go straight	86.3		34.	Go straight	132.2	
			11.5				0.3
16.	Go straight	74.8		33.	Turn right	131.9	
			7.4				0.8
15.	Go straight	67.4		32.	Turn left	131.1	
			1.3				0.4
14.	Go straight	66.1		31.	Turn right	130.7	
			12.7				0.6
13.	Go straight	53.4		30.	Turn left	130.1	
			6.6				0.9
12.	Go straight	46.8		29.	Go straight	129.2	
			9.7				0.2
11.	Go straight	37.1		28.	Go straight	129.0	
			6.6				0.6
10.	Go straight	30.5		27.	Go straight	128.4	
			0.5				3.3
9.	Go straight	30.0		26.	Go straight	127.4	
			4.2				0.1
8.	Go straight	25.8		25.	Go straight	126.2	
			7.6				0.9
7.	Go straight	18.2		24.	Go straight	125.3	
			2.5				1.3
6.	Go straight	15.7		23.	Go straight	124.0	
			2.4				0.5
5.	Go straight	13.3		22.	Go straight	123.5	
			4.0				1.1
4.	Go straight	9.3		21.	Turn left	122.4	
			4.6				1.6
3.	Go straight	4.7		20.	Go straight	120.8	
			2.4				2.6
2.	Go straight	2.3		19.	Go straight	118.2	
			2.3				2.8
1.	Start	0					

139

RAS AL KHOR (KHAWR) WILDLIFE SANCTUARY

Encircled by the bustling metropolis of Dubai lies a haven for thousands of flamingos. The Ras Al Khor (Khawr) Wildlife Sanctuary is the first in a series of parks planned by the Environment Department of Dubai Municipality. Work has already started on the Jebel Ali Wildlife Sanctuary on the coast and others are planned in the desert near Al Awir and in the mountains near Hatta.

The Ras Al Khor sanctuary is located at the end of Dubai Creek in the shallow buffer zone. It stands on a total area of 6.2 sq km on your left hand side as you leave Dubai. To reach the sanctuary from the feeder routes out of Dubai, you take the Hatta road to loop round the Bin Khidra Interchange and get to the car park. From the car park you can walk to a viewing hide allowing you to get a closer view without disturbing the wildlife. On most days a large number of lesser and greater flamingos can be seen in the creek. The sanctuary is home to 266 species of fauna, including curlew, heron, plover, Common Kingfisher, Terek Sandpiper and many other migratory birds including 4,000 broad-billed sandpipers which arrive in autumn. There are more than 1,000 resident flamingos all year round and this number rises to 2,000 in winter. There are also 47 species of flora, including mangroves. The tidal flats support a rich population of invertebrates, a source of food for the multitude of birds that turn the area into a vital roosting site for winter. The sanctuary also has mammals including cape hares and foxes.

The Ras Al Khor (Khawr) Wildlife Sanctuary is open from 9am to 4pm Saturday to Thursday, but is currently closed on a Friday.

DUBAI TO HATTA (E44)

I have chosen to follow the **E44** to Hatta. Some may find it quicker to go down the **E66** then take the **E77** turn off to Lahbab and join the **E44** there. Hatta is a nice easy drive and there are a number of interesting things to do and see in Hatta without even going to Hatta Pools. One can also get to the East Coast from Hatta following the Hatta to Fujairah route on page 71.

1. The route starts where the **E66** (Oud Metha Road) crosses over the **E11** opposite Wafi City.
2. Go straight through the roundabout (1st exit) and continue along Oud Metha Road. On your left hand side at the end of Dubai creek a large number of flamingos can be seen in the Ras Al Khor (Khawr) Wildlife and Waterbird Sanctuary.
3. Take the feed road to Hatta and Oman at the Bin Khidra inter-change.
4. Take the left fork for Hatta and Oman. The right fork takes you to Jebel Ali and Abu Dhabi.
5. Take the off ramp on the right for Hatta and Oman **E44**.
6. Go straight past the turning for Jebel Ali take this turning to get back to the bird hide at Ras Al Khor (Khawr) wildlife sanctuary. You will shortly merge with the **E44**.
7. Go straight past the turning for Ras Al Khor.
8. Go straight past the turning for Al Rashidiya. Take this turning to get back to the second bird hide at Ras Al Khor (Khawr) wildlife sanctuary.
9. Go straight past the turning for the **E311**. You can take this to get to Dubai Airport or to Jebel Ali and Abu Dhabi.
10. Go straight through the next roundabout. You can turn right for Academic City.
11. At the next roundabout go straight. You can turn left onto the **E611** to Sharjah and Al Dhaid. This is the route used to Masafi page 148.
12. Go straight through the roundabout.
13. Go straight at the next roundabout. You can turn right here onto the **E77** for Jebel Ali and Abu Dhabi. At the time of writing the road to Hatta was signposted incorrectly as **E77** at the roundabout exit.
14. Go straight past the turning for Margham.

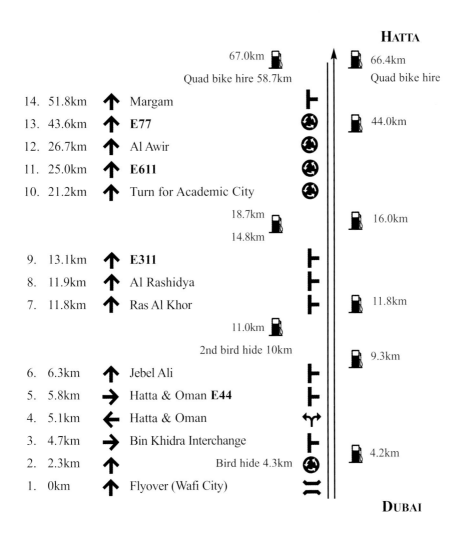

HATTA

67.0km

66.4km

Quad bike hire 58.7km

Quad bike hire

14. 51.8km — Margam

13. 43.6km — **E77**

44.0km

12. 26.7km — Al Awir

11. 25.0km — **E611**

10. 21.2km — Turn for Academic City

18.7km

16.0km

14.8km

9. 13.1km — **E311**

8. 11.9km — Al Rashidya

7. 11.8km — Ras Al Khor

11.8km

11.0km

2nd bird hide 10km

9.3km

6. 6.3km — Jebel Ali

5. 5.8km → Hatta & Oman **E44**

4. 5.1km ← Hatta & Oman

3. 4.7km → Bin Khidra Interchange

4.2km

2. 2.3km — Bird hide 4.3km

1. 0km — Flyover (Wafi City)

DUBAI

143

15.   Go straight at the Madam R/A following the sign to Hatta. You can turn left here onto the **E55** for Meliha, Dhaid and then on to Fujairah on the **E88** or right to Shwaib and onto Al Ain on the **E66**.

16.   Go straight through the roundabout. Turn left here for Mahdah and on to Al Ain. This is the road used by the Al Ain to Hatta route on page 59.

17.   Go straight across the bridge. Just after the bridge is a carpet and pot souq that stretches sporadically from here to Hatta. Be prepared to bargain hard.

18.   At the Hatta Fort Roundabout turn left for Hatta Fort Hotel. Turn right to go into Hatta and the start of the route to Hatta Pools. Carrying straight on will take you to Oman and the border post.

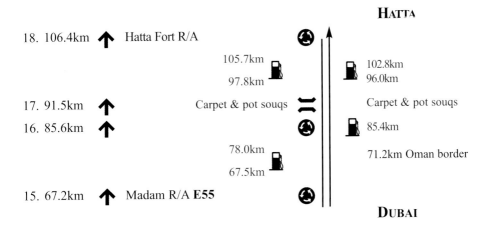

HATTA

18. 106.4km ↑ Hatta Fort R/A

105.7km
97.8km

102.8km
96.0km

17. 91.5km ↑ Carpet & pot souqs

Carpet & pot souqs

16. 85.6km ↑

85.4km

78.0km
67.5km

71.2km Oman border

15. 67.2km ↑ Madam R/A **E55**

DUBAI

ROUTE KILOMETRES

STEP	ACTION	KM	DISTANCE KM	STEP	ACTION	KM	DISTANCE KM
9.	Go straight	13.1		18.	End	106.4	
			1.2				14.9
8.	Go straight	11.9		17.	Go straight	91.5	
			0.1				5.9
7.	Turn left	11.8		16.	Go straight	85.6	
			5.5				48.4
6.	Turn right	6.3		15.	Turn left	67.2	
			0.5				15.4
5.	Go straight	5.8		14.	Go straight	51.8	
			0.7				8.2
4.	Go straight	5.1		13.	Turn right	43.6	
			0.4				6.9
3.	Go straight	4.7		12.	Turn right	26.7	
			2.4				1.7
2.	Turn left	2.3		11.	Turn left	25.0	
			2.3				3.8
1.	Start	0		10.	Go straight	21.2	
							8.1

SHARJAH DESERT PARK, ARABIAN WILDLIFE CENTRE AND NATURAL HISTORY MUSEUM

Located just outside Sharjah is the Sharjah Desert Park, which includes the Arabian Wildlife Centre and Natural History Museum. The turning for the Desert Park is at point 15 on the DUBAI TO MASAFI route. The park is located about 26 km from the centre of the city after the Sharjah International Airport at Interchange No. 9.

The Natural History Museum has five main exhibition halls. The first, "A Journey Through Sharjah" depicts the variety of habitat ranging from desert areas to the more temperate mountainous areas and coastline. The "Man and Environment" exhibition depicts the environmental development of the area and the impact of man.The mechanical camel in this exhibit is particularly popular with young visitors. The third exhibit, "A Journey Through Time" contains fascinating geological samples as well as a two hour video outlining the story of the earth from the beginning of time. "The Living Desert" exhibit includes a garden with a multitude of desert and wadi plants, while "The Living Sea" exhibit houses replicas of sea creatures and habitats.

The Arabian Wildlife Centre is home to a broad range of Arabian fauna, including species that are common like numerous lizards, rodents and snakes, uncommon like the Ruppell's Fox and Sand cat, seriously endangered like the Arabian leopard, or extinct on the Arabian peninsular like the jackal and cheetah. The large aviary where birds fly freely depicts a life-like desert habitat, while Arabian oryx, goat, gazelle and ostrich graze peacefully under the palm trees in an outdoor enclosure. The centre also includes a reptile and insect house as well as a nocturnal house where the visitor can view creatures like the mongoose, foxes, porcupine and many others.The children's farm allows close contact with farm animals.

The centre provides an enjoyable day out for the whole family with its picnic spots and cafeterias and permits a close encounter with a range of desert creatures which are rarely sighted by the casual observer.

Sharjah Natural History Museum & Desert Park
P.O. Box 25313
Sharjah, United Arab Emirates
Tel: 06 5311411 Fax: 06 5311012

Arabian Wildlife Centre
P.O. Box 2926, Sharjah, United Arab Emirates
Tel: 06 5311999 Fax: 06 5311419
Entry: Adults Dhs.15, Children under 16 free.

Opening Times: 09:00 - 17:30
Thursdays: 11:00 - 17:30, Fridays: 14:00 - 17:30, Closed on Monday.

DUBAI TO MASAFI

The route to Masafi takes you to the start of the route to Fujairah (page 77). This route avoids driving along the **E11** through Dubai and Sharjah to the **E88**, but rather takes the **E44** then the **E611** bypass to the **E88** then on to Masafi, thus avoiding the traffic between Dubai and Sharjah. This route also passes the start of the SHARJAH TO KHOR KALBA route (page 93), Sharjah Desert Park, The Natural History Museum and the Friday Market just before Masafi. Although it is called Friday Market, it is open every day. It has a selection of carpet stalls, fruit stalls as well as a few plant stalls.

1. The route starts where the **E66** (Oud Metha Road) crosses over the **E11** opposite Wafi City.
2. Go straight through the roundabout (1st exit) and continue along Oud Metha Road. On your left hand side at the end of Dubai creek a large number of flamingos can be seen in the Ras Al Khor (Khawr) Wildlife and Waterbird Sanctuary.
3. Take the feed road to Hatta and Oman at the Bin Khidra interchange.
4. Take the left fork for Hatta and Oman. The right fork takes you to Jebel Ali and Abu Dhabi.
5. Take the off ramp on the right for Hatta and Oman **E44**.
6. Go straight past the turning for Jebel Ali, take this turning to get back to the bird hide at Ras Al Khor (Khawr) wildlife sanctuary. You will shortly merge with the **E44**.
7. Go straight past the turning for Ras Al Khor.
8. Go straight past the turning for Al Rashidiya. Take this turning to get back to the second bird hide at Ras Al Khor (Khawr) wildlife sanctuary.
9. Go straight past the turning for the **E311**. You can take this to get to Dubai Airport or to Jebel Ali and Abu Dhabi.
10. Go straight through the next roundabout. You can turn right for Academic City.
11. At the next roundabout turn left onto the **E611** to Sharjah and Al Dhaid.
12. Go straight through the next roundabout.
13. Go straight. Turning right here is the start of the route to Khor Kalba (page 93).
14. Go straight across the flyover.
15. Go straight past the turning for Sharjah
16. Turn right onto the **E88** to Al Dhaid and Al Fujairah.
17. Go straight under interchange 8.
18. Go straight under interchange 9. Turn here for Sharjah Desert Park, Natural History Museum, Arabian Wildlife Centre and Arab Cultural Monument.
19. Go straight under interchange 10 the turning for Al Muntathir.

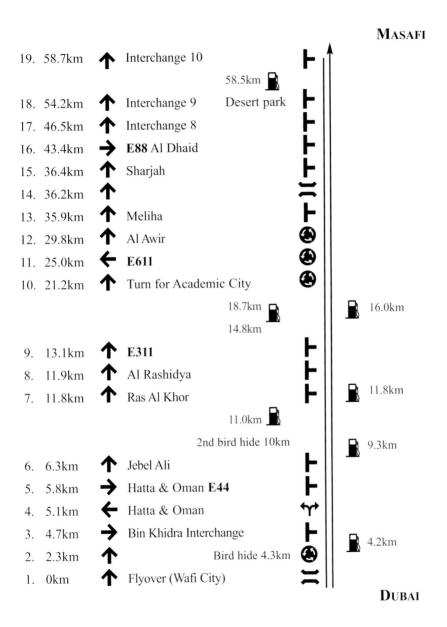

MASAFI

19. 58.7km ⬆ Interchange 10

    58.5km (fuel) 58.5km

18. 54.2km ⬆ Interchange 9   Desert park

17. 46.5km ⬆ Interchange 8

16. 43.4km ➡ **E88** Al Dhaid

15. 36.4km ⬆ Sharjah

14. 36.2km ⬆

13. 35.9km ⬆ Meliha

12. 29.8km ⬆ Al Awir

11. 25.0km ⬅ **E611**

10. 21.2km ⬆ Turn for Academic City

    18.7km (fuel)   16.0km

    14.8km

9. 13.1km ⬆ **E311**

8. 11.9km ⬆ Al Rashidya

7. 11.8km ⬆ Ras Al Khor   11.8km

    11.0km (fuel)

    2nd bird hide 10km   9.3km

6. 6.3km ⬆ Jebel Ali

5. 5.8km ➡ Hatta & Oman **E44**

4. 5.1km ⬅ Hatta & Oman

3. 4.7km ➡ Bin Khidra Interchange

2. 2.3km ⬆   Bird hide 4.3km   4.2km

1. 0km ⬆ Flyover (Wafi City)

DUBAI

149

20.   Go straight under interchange 11.
21.   Go straight under interchange 12 the turning for Tawi Al Saman.
22.   Go across the bridge.
23.   At the next roundabout Hisn Square turn left
24.   At the next roundabout Mosque Square turn right.
25.   Go straight though the oval roundabout you are now on the **E89**.
26.   Go straight past the turning for Al Siji.
27.   Go straight past the turning for Manama.
28.   Go straight past the Friday Market on either side of the road.
29.   Go straight across a bridge.
30.   Go straight across a bridge.
31.   Go straight past the turning for Marbad.
32.   You have reached the end of the route. You can turn left at the roundabout on the **E89** and head to Dibba or turn right on the **E89** to Fujairah. Turning right is the start of the route to Fujairah on page 77.

ROUTE KILOMETRES

STEP	ACTION	KM	DISTANCE KM	STEP	ACTION	KM	DISTANCE KM
16.	Go right	43.4		32.	End	105.3	
			7.0				3.4
15.	Go straight	36.4		31.	Go straight	101.9	
			0.2				0.4
14.	Go straight	36.2		30.	Go straight	101.5	
			0.3				1.3
13.	Go straight	35.9		29.	Go straight	100.2	
			6.1				1.3
12.	Go straight	29.8		28.	Go straight	98.9	
			4.8				10.3
11.	Turn left	25.0		27.	Go straight	88.6	
			3.8				2.1
10.	Go straight	21.2		26.	Go straight	86.5	
			8.1				9.0
9.	Go straight	13.1		25.	Go straight	77.5	
			1.2				3.4
8.	Go straight	11.9		24.	Go right	74.1	
			0.1				0.8
7.	Go straight	11.8		23.	Go left	73.3	
			5.5				1.3
6.	Go straight	6.3		22.	Go straight	72.0	
			0.5				5.0
5.	Turn right	5.8		21.	Go straight	67.0	
			0.7				2.8
4.	Take left fork	5.1		20.	Go straight	64.2	
			0.4				5.5
3.	Turn right	4.7		19.	Go straight	58.7	
			2.4				4.5
2.	Go straight	2.3		18.	Go straight	54.2	
			2.3				7.7
1.	Start	0		17.	Go straight	46.5	
							3.1

MASAFI

32. 105.3km ↑ End   Masafi Police Station ⊛   🅿 104.9km

                                        104.7km 🅿

31. 101.9km ↑
30. 101.5km ↑
29. 100.2km ↑

                             99.6km 🅿

28. 98.9km ↑   Friday Market   Friday Market

                             89.8km 🅿

27. 88.6km ↑ Manama
26. 86.5km ↑ Al Siji   🅿 86.4km

                             85.7km 🅿

25. 77.5km ↑ Masafi **E89**

                             75.3km 🅿   🅿 74.9km

24. 74.1km → Mosque Square

                             73.9km 🅿

23. 73.3km ← Hisn Square   🅿 72.9km
22. 72.0km ↑

                             71.3km 🅿

21. 67.0km ↑ Interchange 12
20. 64.2km ↑ Interchange 11

                                        DUBAI

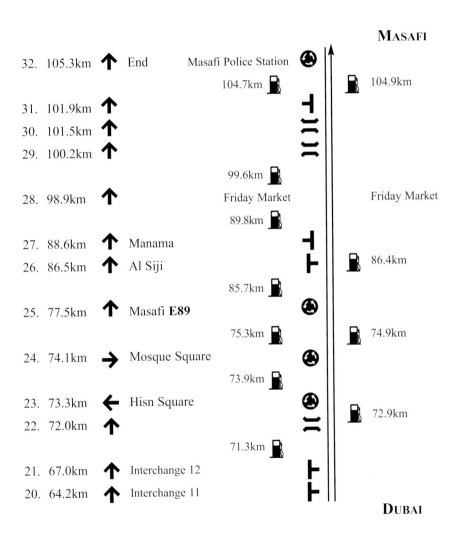

151

ROUTE KEY & SYMBOL LEGEND

→	Tar road	◉	Photo opportunity
⇒	Duel-carriageway	←	Turn left
---►	Dirt road	→	Turn right
⊢	T-junction to the right	↑	Straight on
⊣	T-junction to the left	⊕	Roundabout
+	Cross roads	⊤	T-junction
Y	Fork	P	Car park
⋒	Tunnel	••••	Wadi crossing
≈	Bridge	≋	Water, possible swimming
⌂	Mosque	⛽	Petrol station
⌃	Oasis	⛫	Fort/watch tower
⋒	U-turn		

HUMAN HISTORY IN THE UAE

The UAE has been inhabited since the late Stone Age 5500 BC and evidence of settlements from this period reveal that the climate was probably wetter than it is today. Stone tools and arrow heads indicate hunting activity on open grasslands which are now desert dunes. Flint tools have been found mainly on natural flint outcrops and in wadi gravel terraces near Al Ain for example Mazyed near Hili and Bida bint Saud. From 3100-3000 BC, sophisticated forms of building developed like the above-ground stone tombs at Jebel Hafeet near Al Ain and Jebel al-Emalah south of Dhaid. Pottery imported from south-central Iraq found in these tombs and the similarity of other artifacts found to those in Egypt at the time indicates widespread trade. The rich resources of copper in the Hajar Mountains were probably one reason for this communication with the outside world during the Bronze Age. This focus on trade is still a trademark of the UAE with Dubai developing into the region's shopping mecca. Around 3000 BC an arid climate, similar to that of today set in. During this time, oasis towns protected by circular fortresses were established probably as protection during conflict over scarce resources. In this period, the dead were buried in round stone communal tombs like those found at Hili. In the Iron Age, the date palm with its multiple uses as well as the development of channeling mechanisms (aflaj) to convey water from mountain sources to small farms and gardens developed the oasis into a haven against the harsh desert climate. In addition, the domestication of the camel provided a form of transport between these pockets of green and the outside world and effectively changed the economy of the area by further widening possible trade routes. The Islamic era in the UAE started in 630 AD with the arrival of envoys from the Prophet Muhammad (Peace Be Upon Him). Many converts were won, but the death of the Holy Prophet in 632 AD was followed by a revolt until the armies of the first Caliph, Abu Bakr won a decisive battle at Dibba, on the UAE's East Coast. Over 10,000 rebels died and most of Arabia returned to Islam. The rebels' graves can still be seen on the outskirts of the town. The sites of Jumairah near Dubai and Julfar in Ras Al Khaimah are the most famous early Islamic sites in the UAE.

Archaeological evidence shows that these medieval cities had contact with countries as far as China, Korea and Thailand. Despite peaceful trade with the outside world, the history of this part of Arabia continued to be bloody, but now it was the influence of foreign invaders that would shape the region for more than three hundred years. The arrival of the Portuguese in the Gulf resulted in conflict for the Arab populations

155

of East Coast ports like Dibba, Bidiya, Khor Fakkan and Kalba. Forts were established in these towns to protect local Arab sheikhs who were allies of the Portuguese from their Omani neighbours of the Ya'ruba Dynasty who were resisting them. In 1650 the Portuguese were removed from Oman by Imam Sultan bin Saif and Oman became the power in the area extending its influence as far as Bahrain. However, civil war and conflict with Persia weakened Oman, allowing the emergence of the Qawasim from Sharjah and Ras Al Khaimah. Meanwhile, the Bani Yas, the ancestors of the bedouin, had settled in Abu Dhabi and Dubai. They created date gardens and built date frond houses in the hollows of the dunes where adequate water was found. The villages at Liwa were vital to the economic and social life for the Bani Yas. However, by the early 1790s the political leader of all the Bani Yas groups moved from Liwa to the town of Abu Dhabi. Early in the nineteenth century, members of the Al Bu Falasah, a branch of the Bani Yas, settled by the Creek in Dubai and established the Maktoum dynasty in that emirate. European powers like Portugal, Holland and later Britain battled for supremacy in the region. But it was the power of the Qawasim, which gave Britain its most serious challenge in its mission to become the dominant power in the Indian Ocean. During the early nineteenth century there were a series of clashes between these two sides which culminated in the defeat of the Qasimi fleet and the strengthening of British influence in the Gulf. The British claimed that the Qasimi vessels had engaged in piracy, thus the area was dubbed: 'The Pirate Coast' and the British were given an excuse for their offensive. However, it is more likely that the reason for this British offensive was their desire to control the sea routes between the

Gulf and India. After the defeat of the Qawasim, the British signed
agreements with the sheikhs of the individual emirates and later joint treaties,
which resulted in the area becoming known as 'The Trucial States'. Peace in
the region resulted in a more widespread exploitation of the pearl fisheries in
the Gulf, and high quality pearls from the emirates were exported to India as
well as Europe. The pearling industry thrived during the nineteenth and early
twentieth centuries, providing one of the main sources of income and
employment to the people of what is now the UAE. The first cargo of crude
oil exported from Abu Dhabi in 1962, changed the economy of the UAE
irrevocably. Every year the revenues have grown, as oil production has
increased. At the beginning of 1968, the British announced their planned
withdrawal from the Arabian Gulf by the end of 1971. H.H.Sheikh Zayed the
ruler of Abu Dhabi took the lead in calling for a federation that would include
not only the seven emirates that together made up the Trucial States, but also
Qatar and Bahrain. However agreement was reached between the rulers of
only six of the emirates (Abu Dhabi, Dubai, Sharjah, Umm al Qaiwain,
Fujairah and Ajman) and the United Arab Emirates (UAE) was formally
established on December 1971.The seventh emirate, Ras Al Khaimah,
formally joined the new federation on 10 February 1972. Under the leadership
of H.H. Sheikh Zayed, the UAE rapidly developed. For example, the
provision of free water to farmers resulted in the development of over 2000
farms in Abu Dhabi, making that Emirate virtually self-sufficient in terms of
fresh produce. Other achievements include the development of an excellent
network of roads cris-crossing the UAE, inspiring the writing of this book. In
November 2004, H.H. Sheikh Khalifa bin Zayed succeeded his father as ruler
of Abu Dhabi and president of the United Arab Emirates.

NATURE IN THE UAE

You may be surprised to discover that a place as dry as the UAE is teeming with wildlife. Unfortunately, for the casual observer, it is not always that easy to see.

You are most likely to see domesticated animals like goats, donkeys and camels on your travels around the UAE. There are no wild camels in the UAE. They all belong to someone, even if they seem to be wondering aimlessly in the desert. One should be particularly careful when driving past camels on the side of the road. Not only will they do a lot of damage to your car if you hit one, but you will also have to contend with a very angry owner, as a camel can be worth a lot of money. In the cities, you will see many thin and unusual looking feral cats. Avoid feeding them, as they can become pests. The UAE is known as a good bird watching spot. In autumn and spring the local bird population grows significantly when migrating birds stop over on their way from Africa and Europe to Asia. Dubai has thousands of flamingos inhabiting an area of swampy land along Oud Metha Road. You can also see parakeets, shrikes, doves, Indian rollers, common mynah, black-crowned finch lark, hoopoe, humes wheatear, socotra cormorants, white cheeked bulbul, Egyptian vultures and little green bee-eaters. The mangrove swamp of Khor Kalba is the only home in the world to the Khor Kalba white-collared kingfisher.

If you are very lucky, you may see some of the mammals that inhabit the UAE, although some are so rarely sighted that they were thought until recently to be extinct. The Arabian leopard, Arabian red fox, Arabian tahr, three types of Arabian hedgehog, capre hare, caracal, Cheesman's gerbil, Gordon's wildcat, mountain gazelle and the mouse-tailed bat all inhabit the UAE. Reptiles thrive in the desert and rocky hills. However, you are unlikely to see many, unless you look very carefully, as some of them have excellent camouflage.

BASIC ARABIC

VOWELS

Approximate English equivalent	Shown below as
a as in 'hat' (short)	*a*
o as in 'know'	*ow*
a as in 'car' (long)	*aa*
oo as in 'boot'	*oo*
ae as in 'aeroplane'	*ae*
i as in 'hit'	*i*
o as in 'doll'	*o*
ee as in 'keen'	*ee*

Other compound vowel sounds used are:

ai as in 'aisle'	*ai*
e as in 'egg'	*e*
ay as in 'day'	*ay*
e-oo	*ew*
ow as in 'now'	*aw*

BASIC WORDS	**ARABIC**
Thanks	shokran
I do not have	maa'indee
You're welcome	afwaan
There isn't any	ma'afee
Please	min fadlak (m), min fadliki (f)
How much?	bikaem?
Okay, lovely, good	zayn
I am sorry	ana aesif
Yes	aywa
And	wa
No	la'a

GREETINGS	**ARABIC**
Greeting (Peace be upon you)	assalaam alaykom
Response (On you be peace)	walaykom assalaam
Good evening	misa' il kheer

160

Good evening in response
How are you?
Good morning
Good morning in response
Fine thank you
Goodbye

misa' innor
kayfhalak (m), kayfhalek (f)
sabah il kheer
sabah innor
ilHamdoolilla
ma a assalaema

INTRODUCTIONS
My name is . . .
What is your name?
Where are you from?
I am from. . .
Africa
America
Australia
Britain
Europe
India

ARABIC
ismi . . .
shoo ismak (m), shoo ismik (f)
inta/inti min ay balaed?
ana min. . .
Afriqiah
Amreekah
Ostralia
Bareetaania
Awropah
Alhind

DIRECTIONS
Excuse me
Where are we?
First
Second
Street
Can you repeat that, please?
Roundabout
Signals
More slowly, please
Close to
Petrol Station
Can I swim here?
Sea / Beach
Mountain
Left
Desert
Right
Airport
Straight
Hotel
Turning

ARABIC
law samaht/samahti
ihna fayn?
awil
taeni
shaeri a
taeni min fadlak/ fadlik?
darwaraan
ishaara
bishwaysh min fadlak/fadlik
orayyib min
mahattit betrol
momkin a a oom hena
it bahr
jabal
yesaar
at sahara
yemeen
mataar
seedaa
foondooq
maafraaq

161

Restaurant | mata'am

ACCIDENTS — ARABIC
Police — al shoortaa
Sorry — aesif (m), aessifa(f)
Permit / license — rokhsa
Accident — Haadsaa
doctor — tabib
Papers — waraíaq
hospital — mostashfa
Insurance — ta'meen
I need help — Bidi musaada

QUESTIONS — ARABIC
How many/much? — kam?
Why? — laysh?
Who? — meen?
Where? — wayn?
How? — kayf?
When? — mta?
To/for — ila
Which? — ay
In/at — fi
What? — shoo?
From — min

NUMBERS	ARABIC	NUMBERS	ARABIC
Zero	sefr	10	ashra
One	wahid	20	ishreen
Two	itnaeyn	30	talaeteen
Three	talaeta	40	arba'een
Four	arba'a	50	khamseen
Five	khamsa	60	seteen
Six	seta	70	saba'en
Seven	saba'a	80	tamaneen
Eight	tamanya	90	tesa'een
Nine	tes a'a	100	maya
		1000	alf

USEFUL PHONE NUMBERS

AREA CODES

Abu Dhabi	02
Al Ain	03
Dubai	04
Ajman	06
UAQ	06
Sharjah	06
RAK	07
Fujairah	09
Khor Fakkan	09
Kalba	09
Mobile	050

EMERGENCY NUMBERS

Police & Emergency	999
Ambulance Services	998
Fire Rescue	997
Operator + Enquiries	181

AMUSEMENT PARKS

Al Ain	Hili Fun City	784 5542
Dubai	Wild Wadi	348 4444
UAQ	Dreamland Aqua Park	768 1888

CAMEL RIDING

Al Ain	Al Ain Camel Safaris	768 8006
Dubai	Mushrif Park	288 3624
	Arabian Adventures	303 4888
Sharjah	Orient Tours	568 2323

DHOW TRIPS

Abu Dhabi	Sunshine Tours	444 9914
Dubai	Coastline Leisure	398 4867
	Danat Dubai	351 1117
	Emirates Travel	286 5758

DIVING

Abu Dhabi	Abu Dhabi Sub Aqua Club	673 1111
	Abu Dhabi Tourist Club	672 3400
	Blue Dolphin Company LLC	666 6888
	Golden Boats	666 8888
	Marina Divers	677 5687
	Scuba International Abu Dhabi	679 0377

163

	Scuba Sheraton	677 3333
	Sirenia	645 4512
UAQ	Dreamland Aqua Park	768 1888
	Sun & Sand Sports	674 6299
	Sun Divers Diving Centre	562 9265
Ajman	Ajman Kempinski Hotel & Resort	745 1555
Dubai	Al Boom Diving	394 1267
	Club Mina	399 3333
	Dubai Sports Diving Club	348 0431
	Emirates Diving Association	393 9390
	Inner Space Diving Centre	393 7775
	Jebel Ali Sailing Club	399 5444
	Lukhma Divers	344 6944
	Oasis Beach Club	399 4444
	Pavilion Dive Centre	348 0000
	Scuba Dubai	331 7433
	Scuba International	393 7557
	Scubatec	334 8988
	Sun & Sand Sports (Deira City Centre)	295 5551
	Sun & Sand Sports (Jumeira)	349 5820
Fujairah	East Coast Outdoor Activities	050 649 9858
	Sandy Beach Diving Centre	244 5050
	Scuba 2000	238 8477
Khor Fakkan	Ocean Divers' Centre	238 5111
	Seven Seas Diving Centre	238 7400
RAK	Sun & Sand Sports	227 9993
Sharjah	Geco Marine	533 0206
	Pearl Marine Sports Centre	5663626
	Sharjah Dive Club	5357505
	Sun & Sand Sports	5727811

HIKING

Dubai	Desert Rangers	346 0808

HORSE RIDING

Abu Dhabi	Abu Dhabi Equestrian Club	445 5500
Al Ain	Inter-Continental Al Ain Riding Stables	768 6686
Dubai	Dubai Equestrian Centre	336 1394
	Jebel Ali Equestrian Club	050 658 7387
	Nad Al Sheba Racecourse	336 3666
Hatta	Hatta Fort Hotel	852 3211
Jebel Ali	Club Joumana	883 6000

MOUNTAIN BIKING

Dubai	Biking Frontiers (Group)	050 552 7300
	Desert Rangers (Tour Operator)	346 0808

ROCK CLIMBING
Dubai	Pyramids	324 0000

CAR RECOVERY SERVICES
Dubai	AAA Service Centre	285 8989
		347 0400
	Arabian Automobile Association	266 9989

CAR RENTALS
Abu Dhabi	Budget Rent-A-Car	633 4200
	Avis	621 8400
	Diamond Lease	677 0699
	Europecar	631 9922
	Hertz Rent a Car	672 0060
	Fast Rent a Car	632 4000
	Thrifty Car Rental	634 5663
	Tourist Rent a Car	641 8700
Dubai	Autolease Rent-a-Car	282 6565
	Avis Rent a Car	295 7121
	Budget Rent-A-Car	295 6667
	Diamondlease Rent-A-Car	331 3172
	Europecar (Dubai Rent-A-Car)	339 4433
	Hertz Rent a Car	282 4422
	Thrifty Car Rental	337 0743
	United Car Rentals	266 6286
Fujairah	Autolease Rent-a-Car	224 2475
	Diamond Lease	223 2885
Sharjah	Autolease Rent-A-Car	573 5333
	Avis	559 5925
	Budget Rent-A-Car	572 7600
	Hertz Rent a Car	572 1527

MUSEUMS & HERITAGE
Abu Dhabi	Cultural Foundation	621 5300
	Handicrafts Centre	447 6645
	Petroleum Exhibition	626 0817
	Women's Handicraft Centre	447 6645
Ajman	Ajman Museum	742 3824
Al Ain	Al Ain Museum	764 1595
	Al Ain University Natural History Museum	761 2277
	Al Ain Zoo & Aquarium	782 8188
Dubai	Dubai Museum	353 1862
	Heritage & Diving Village	393 7151
	Majlis Ghorfat Urn Al Sheef	394 6343
	Museum for Children	336 9082
	Museum of Education	226 0286

165

	Sheikh Saeed Al Maktoumís House	393 7139
	Sheikh Mohammed Centre for	344 7755
	Cultural Understanding	
	Open Zoo	349 6444
	Zoo	344 0462
Fujairah	Fujairah Heritage Village	222 7000
	Fujairah Museum	222 9085
Kalba	Al Hesen Museum	277 4442
RAK	National Museum of RAK	233 3411
Sharjah	AI Hisn Fort/Heritage Museum	568 5500
	Arabia's Wildlife Centre	531 1999
	Children's Farm	531 1411
	Discovery Centre	558 6577
	Planetarium, The	528 6227
	Sharjah Archaeological Museum	566 5466
	Sharjah Art Museum	568 8222
	Sharjah Desert Park	531 1411
	Sharjah Heritage Museum	568 1738
	Sharjah Islamic Museum	568 3334
	Sharjah Natural History Museum	531 1411
	Sharjah Science Museum	566 8777

ENVIRONMENTAL GROUPS

Abu Dhabi	Abu Dhabi Emirates Natural History Group	604 3313
	Feline Friends	665 5297
	K9 Friends	359 8208
Al Ain	Al Ain Emirates Natural History Group	768 6686
Dubai	Arabian Leopard Trust	344 4871
	Dubai Natural History Group	349 4816
	Emirates Bird Records Committee	347 2277
	Emirates Diving Association	393 9390
	Feline Friends	050 451 0058
	K9 Friends	3474611

GOVERNMENT DEPARTMENTS

Dubai	Department of Tourism and	
	Commerce Marketing	223 0000
	Marine Environment &Sanctuaries Unit	
	Environment Department	206 4240
Fujairah	Fujairah Tourism Bureau	223 1554
Sharjah	Sharjah Commerce and Tourism	
	Development Authority	5566777

HOSPITALS

Abu Dhabi	Ahlia Hospital	626 2666
	Al Noor Hospital	626 5265

166

	National Hospital	671 1000
Al Ain	Al Ain Hospital	763 5888
	Oasis Hospital	722 1251
	Specialised Medical Care Hospital	755 2291
	Emirates International Hospital	763 7777
Dubai	International Private Hospital	221 2484
	American Hospital	336 7777
	Welcare Hospital	282 7788
	Emirates Hospital	349 6666

HOTELS & MOTELS

Al Ain	Rotana Hotel Al Ain	754 5111
	Hilton Al Ain	768 6666
	Hotel Inter-Continental Al Ain	768 6686
	Mercure Grand Jebel Hafeet	783 8888
Dubai	Al Maha Desert Resort	303 4222
	Bab Al Shams Desert Resort and Spa	832 6699
Fujairah	Fujairah Beach Motel	222 8111
	Fujairah Hilton	222 2411
	Holiday Beach Motel	244 5540
	Ritz Plaza Hotel	222 2202
	Sandy Beach Motel	244 5354
	Le Meridien	244 9000
Kalba	Breeze Motel	277 8877
Hatta	Hatta Fort Hotel	852 3211
Khor Fakkan	Oceanic Hotel	238 5111
Liwa	Liwa Oasis City (Liwa Hotel)	882 2000

MUNICIPALITIES

Abu Dhabi	Abu Dhabi Municipality	678 8888
Dubai	Dubai Municipality	221 5555
	Municipality Hotline	223 2323
Fujairah	Fujairah Municipality	222 7000

TOUR OPERATORS

Abu Dhabi	NetTours	679 4656
	OffRoad Emirates	633 3232
	Orient Tours	667 1760
Al Ain	Al Ain Camel Safaris	768 8006
Dubai	Arabian Adventures	303 4888
	Axis Holidays Worldwide	203 3333
	Columbus Tours	224 2555
	Desert Adventure Tourism	224 2800
	Desert Rangers	346 0808
	Dubai Travel & Tourist Services	343 2221
	Gulf Ventures	209 5509

EMBASSIES

Embassy of America	PO Box 4009, Abu Dhabi	T: 4436691	F: 4434171
Embassy of Australia	PO Box 32711, Abu Dhabi	T: 6346100	
Embassy of Austria	PO Box 3095, Abu Dhabi	T: 6766611	F: 6715551
Embassy of Bahrain	PO Box 3367, Abu Dhabi	T: 6657500	
Embassy of Bangladesh	PO Box 2504, Abu Dhabi	T: 4465100	F: 4667324
Embassy of Belarus	PO Box 30337, Abu Dhabi	T: 4453399	F: 4451131
Embassy of Belgium	PO Box 3686, Abu Dhabi	T: 6319449	F:6319353
Embassy of Bosnia & Herzegovina	PO Box 43362, Abu Dhabi	T: 6444164	
Embassy of Brazil	PO Box 3027, Abu Dhabi	T: 6320606	
Embassy of Brunei	PO Box 5836, Abu Dhabi	T: 4491100	
Embassy of Canada	PO Box 6970, Abu Dhabi	T: 4456969	
Embassy of China	PO Box 2741, Abu Dhabi	T: 4434276	F:4435440
Embassy of Czech Republic	PO Box 27009, Abu Dhabi	T: 6782800	F:6795716
Embassy of Egypt	PO Box 4026 Abu Dhabi	T: 4445566	F: 4449878
Embassy of Finland	PO Box 3634, Abu Dhabi	T: 6328927	F: 6325063
Embassy of France	PO Box 4014, Abu Dhabi	T: 4435100	
Embassy of Germany	PO Box 2591, Abu Dhabi	T: 4435630	F:4435625
Embassy of Greece	PO Box 5483, Abu Dhabi	T: 6654847	F: 6656008
Embassy of Hungary	PO Box 44450, Abu Dhabi	T: 6660107	F: 6667877
Embassy of India	PO Box 737, Abu Dhabi	T: 4492700	F:4444685
Embassy of Indonesia	PO Box 7256, Abu Dhabi	T: 4454448	F: 4455453
Embassy of Italy	PO Box 46752, Abu Dhabi	T: 4435622	F: 4434337
Embassy of Japan	PO Box 2430, Abu Dhabi	T: 4435696	
Embassy of Jordan	PO Box 4024	T: 4447100	F: 4449157
Embassy of Korea	PO Box 3270, Abu Dhabi	T: 4435337	F: 4435348
Embassy of Kuwait	PO Box 926 Abu Dhabi	T: 4446888	F: 4444109
Embassy of Lebanon	PO Box 4023 Abu Dhabi	T: 4492100	
Embassy of Malaysia	PO Box 3887, Abu Dhabi	T: 4482775	
Embassy of Netherlands	PO Box 46560 Abu Dhabi	T: 6321920	F: 6313158
Embassy of Norway	PO Box 47270, Abu Dhabi	T: 6211221	
Embassy of Pakistan	PO Box 846 Abu Dhabi	T: 4447800	F: 4447172
Embassy of Philippines	PO Box 3215, Abu Dhabi	T: 6345664	F: 6313559
Embassy of Poland	PO Box 2334 Abu Dhabi	T: 4465200	F: 4462967
Embassy of Qatar	PO Box 3503, Abu Dhabi	T: 4493300	F: 4493311
Embassy of Romania	PO Box 70416, Abu Dhabi	T: 6666346	
Embassy of Russia	PO Box 8211, Abu Dhabi	T: 6721797	F:6788731
Embassy of Saudi Arabia	PO Box 4057, Abu Dhabi	T: 4445700	F:4446747
Embassy of Slovakia	PO Box 3382, Abu Dhabi	T: 6321674	F: 6315839

Embassy of South Africa	PO Box 29446, Abu Dhabi	T: 6316700	
Embassy of Spain	PO Box 46474, Abu Dhabi	T: 6269544	F: 6274978
Embassy of Sri Lanka	PO Box 46534, Abu Dhabi	T: 6426666	F: 6428289
Embassy of Sultanate of Oman	PO Box 2517, Abu Dhabi	T: 4463333	F: 4464633
Embassy of Sweden	PO Box 47270, Abu Dhabi	T: 6210162	F: 6394941
Embassy of Switzerland	PO Box 46116, Abu Dhabi	T: 6274636	F: 6269627
Embassy of Syria	PO Box 4011, Abu Dhabi	T: 4448768	F: 4443531
Embassy of Thailand	PO Box 47466, Abu Dhabi	T: 6421772	F:6421773/4
Embassy of Ukraine	PO Box 45714, Abu Dhabi	T: 6327586	F: 6327506
Embassy of United Kingdom	PO Box 248, Abu Dhabi	T: 6101100	
Visa/Consular Information		T: 6101122	
Embassy of Yemen	PO Box 2095, Abu Dhabi	T: 4448457	F: 4447978

CONSULATES

British Embassy	PO Box 65, Dubai	T: 3094444	F: 3094301
Consular Agency of Italy	PO Box 9250, Dubai	T: 3314167	F: 3317469
Consulate General of USA	PO Box 9343, Dubai	T: 3116000	
Consulate General of Australia	PO Box 58010, Dubai	T: 3212444	F: 3212677
Consulate General of France	PO Box 3314, Dubai	T: 3329040	F: 3328033
Consulate General of Germany	PO Box 2247, Dubai	T: 3972333	F: 3972225
Consulate General of Japan	PO Box 9336, Dubai	T: 3319191	F: 3319292
Consulate General of Jordan	PO Box 2787, Dubai	T: 3970500	F:3971675
Consulate General of Kuwait	PO Box 806, Dubai	T: 3978000	
Consulate General of Malaysia	PO Box 4598, Dubai	T: 3355528	F: 3352220
Consulate General of New Zealand	PO Box 23156, Dubai	T: 3317500	F: 3317501
Consulate General of Qatar	PO Box 1877, Dubai	T: 3982888	F: 3983555
Consulate General of Romania	PO Box 1404, Dubai	T: 3940580	F: 3940992
Consulate General of Sweden	PO Box 9219, Dubai	T: 3457716	
Consulate General of Thailand	PO Box 51844, Dubai	T: 3492863	F: 3490932
Consulate General of Turkey	PO Box 9221, Dubai	T: 3314788	F: 3317317
Consulate General of Yemen	PO Box 1947, Dubai	T: 3970131	F: 3972901
Consulate of Canada	PO Box 52472, Dubai	T: 3521717	F: 3517722
Consulate of Denmark	PO Box 2988, Dubai	T: 2227699	F: 2235751
Consulate of Netherlands	PO Box 7726, Dubai	T: 3528700	F: 3510502
Consulate of Norway	PO Box 8612, Dubai	T: 3533833	
Consulate of Philippines	PO Box 14066, Dubai	T: 2230903	
Consulate of Russia	PO Box 8211, Dubai	T: 2231272	

Satellite Road Map of the United Arab Emirates

Key

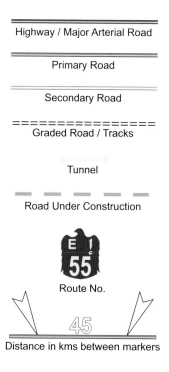

Highway / Major Arterial Road

Primary Road

Secondary Road

Graded Road / Tracks

Tunnel

Road Under Construction

Route No.

Distance in kms between markers

International Airport

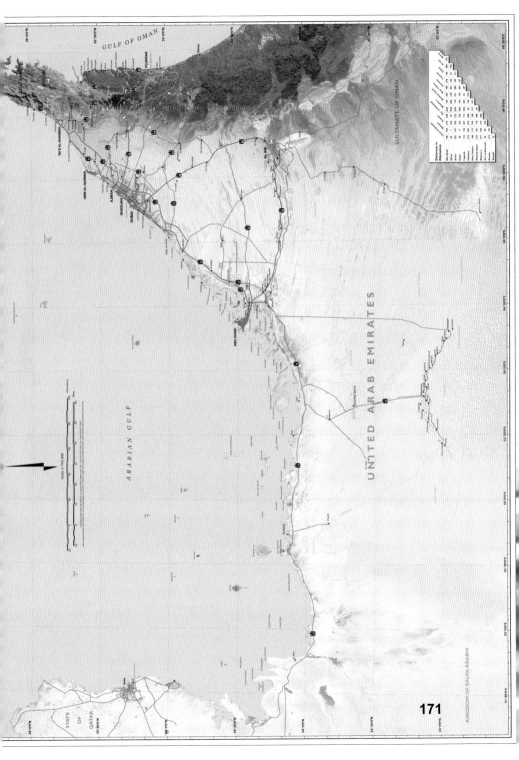

GULF OF OMAN

SULTANATE OF OMAN

ARABIAN GULF

UNITED ARAB EMIRATES

RAS AL-KHAIMAH

UMM AL-QAIWAIN

AJMAN

SHARJAH

DUBAI

ABU DHABI

AL AIN

FUJAIRAH

STATE OF QATAR

KINGDOM OF SAUDI ARABIA

Scale 1:700,000

171

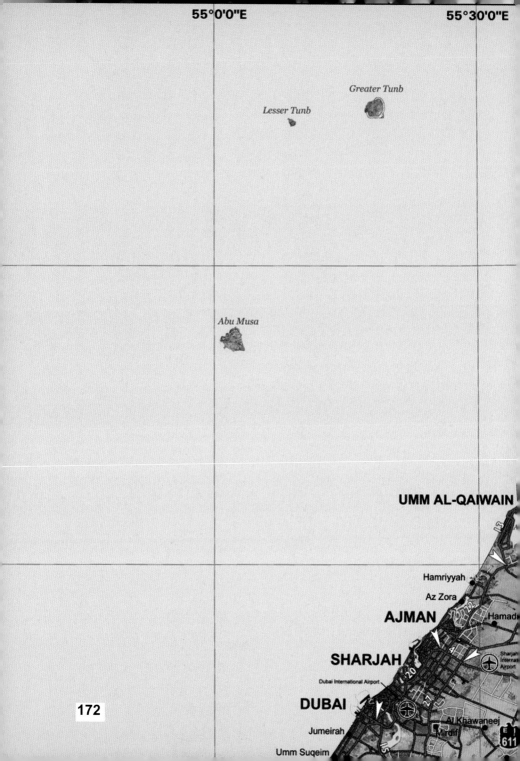

Greater Tunb

Lesser Tunb

Abu Musa

UMM AL-QAIWAIN

Hamriyyah

Az Zora

AJMAN

Hamad

SHARJAH

Sharjah
International
Airport

Dubai International Airport

DUBAI

Jumeirah

Al Khawaneej

Mirdif

Umm Suqeim

611

STRAIT OF HORMUZ

Al Khasab

SULTANATE

OF

OMAN

26°0'0"N

Ghalilah

Port Saqr

E 11

Khor
Al-Khuwair

Ar Rams

Shimal

Mu'ayrid

RA'S AL-KHAIMAH

Al Hamra

Khawran

Hayl
Al Fahlah

Habhab

Digdaga

DAWHAT DIBBA

Dibba

Rul Dibba

Ra's Dibba

Ra's al-Khaimah
International
Airport

Khatt

Rul Dhadnah

Rafah

Hamraniyyah

E 18

Tawiyeen

Dhadnah

Al Aqqah

25°30'0"N

Bathi Mahani

E 87

E 89

Sharm

Adhan

Bidiya

E 55

Tayyibah

Luluyyah

Ghayl

KHOR FAKKAN

Falaj al-Mu'alla

Manama

18

Masafi

Qidfa

Murbah

Dhaid

14

Siji

E 89

Quraayah

18

24

Bithna

E 99

GULF OF OMAN

173

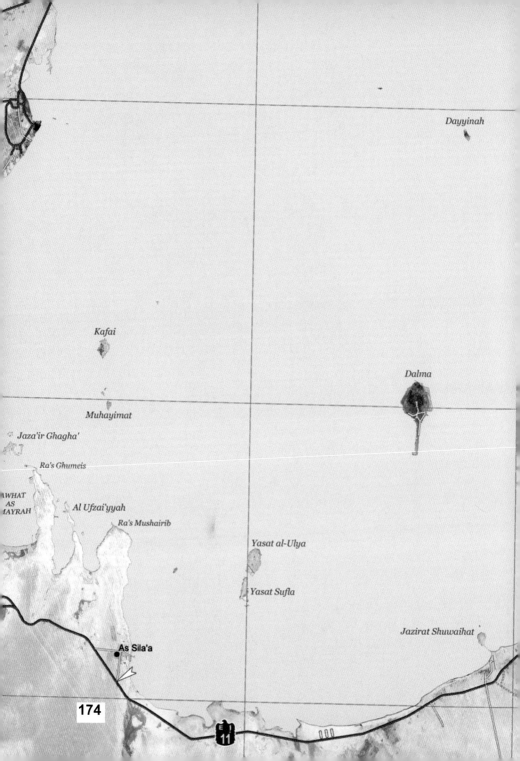

Dayyinah

Kafai

Dalma

Muhayimat

Jaza'ir Ghagha'

Ra's Ghumeis

AWHAT
AS
MAYRAH

Al Ufzai'yyah

Ra's Mushairib

Yasat al-Ulya

Yasat Sufla

Jazirat Shuwaihat

As Sila'a

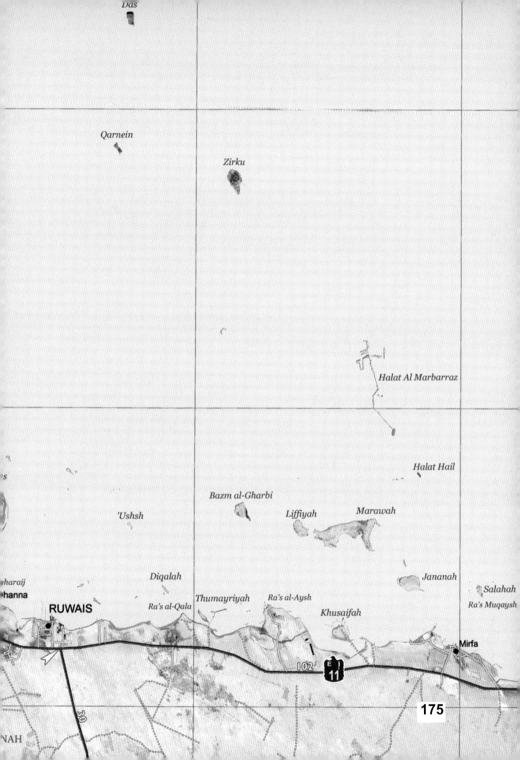

Das

Qarnein

Zirku

Halat Al Marbarraz

Halat Hail

Bazm al-Gharbi

'Ushsh   Liffiyah   Marawah

Jananah

haraij   Diqalah   Salahah
hanna   Ra's Muqaysh
RUWAIS   Ra's al-Qala   Thumayriyah   Ra's al-Aysh
                                                Khusaifah
                                                              Mirfa

102   E 11

175

NAH

DAWHA

H

Ghurab

Ba

KHOR FARIDAH

Sadiyat

Ramka

ABU DHABI

Lulu

Umm al-N

Maqta

17

Al Bahrani

Hudaeriyyat

Al Aryam

Futaisi

MUSAFFAH

Ra's Kahf

KHOR QIRQISHAN

Jam

21

Abu al-Abyadh

Ra's Musejd

Maqatara

Ra's al-Hadrah

Qusabi

ah

Bu Sharah

wshit

Rufayq

KHOR QANTAR

62

E
11

Tarif

176

4

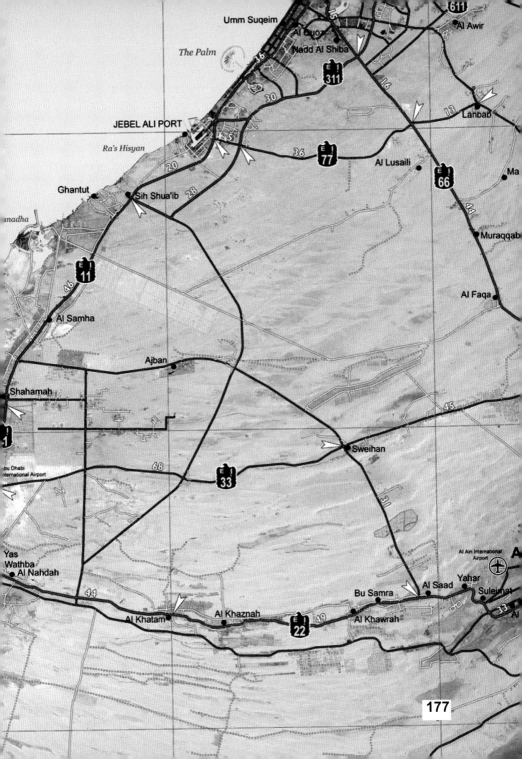

Umm Suqeim

The Palm

Al Quoz

Nadd Al Shiba

E 311

611

Al Awir

Lahbab

16

13

JEBEL ALI PORT

Ra's Hisyan

5

36

E 77

Al Lusaili

E 66

Ma

Ghantut

Sih Shua'ib

20

28

44

Muraqqab

46

E 11

Al Faqa

Al Samha

Ajban

Shahamah

1

Abu Dhabi
International Airport

68

E 33

45

Sweihan

30

Al Ain International
Airport

A

Yas

Wathba

Al Nahdah

44

Yahar

Suleimat

Bu Samra

Al Saad

E 33

Al

Al Khatam

Al Khaznah

E 22

49

Al Khawrah

177

FUJAIRAH

Fujairah International Airport

Kalba

Khor Kalba

Bithna

Margham

Al Madam

Fili

Huwaylat

Al Jizer

Hatta

Shinas

raqqab

Ash Shu'ayb

Hayer

AL AIN

Al 'Oha

Hili

Al Maqam

178 Hafit

BAYNUNAH

Ghiyathi

Bu Hasa

UNITED

43

Khan

K

AL MAGHRIB

Umm Hisin

Arada

180

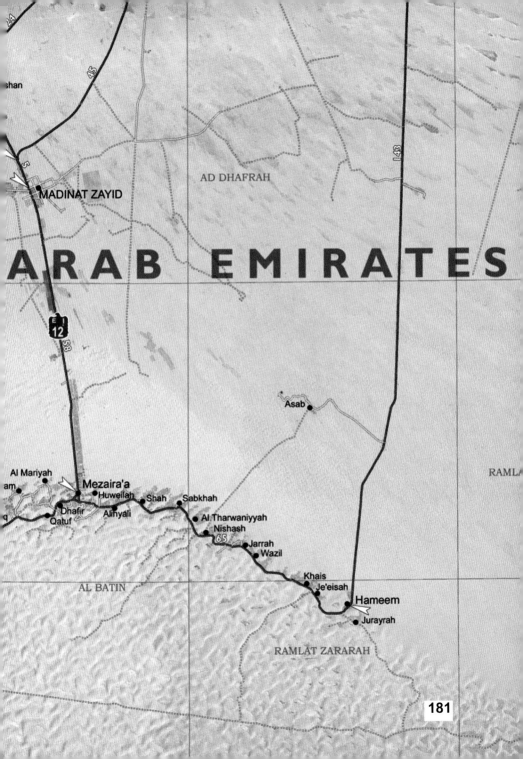

AD DHAFRAH

MADINAT ZAYID

ARAB EMIRATES

E
12
58

Asab

Al Mariyah
Mezaira'a
Huweilah
Shah
Sabkhah
Dhafir
Alihyali
Al Tharwaniyyah
Qatuf
Nishash
65
Jarrah
Wazil

RAMLA

Khais
Je'eisah
Hameem
AL BATIN
Jurayrah

RAMLAT ZARARAH

181

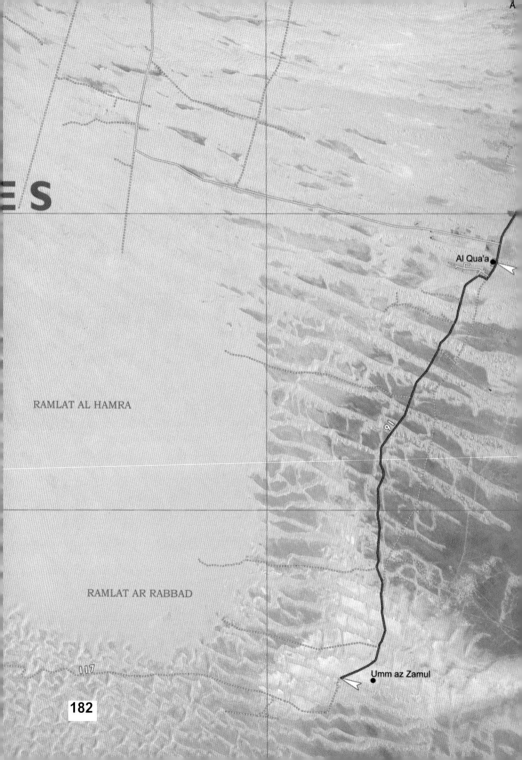

ES

Al Qua'a

RAMLAT AL HAMRA

911

RAMLAT AR RABBAD

117

Umm az Zamul

SULTANATE OF OMAN

23°

Distances in Kilometres	Umm al-Qaiwain	Sharjah	Ruwais	Ra's al-Khaimah	Mezaira'a	Madinat Zayid	Khor Fakkan	Hameem	Fujairah	Dubai	Al Ain	Ajman
Abu Dhabi	196	164	234	249	222	142	304	166	278	145	160	170
Ajman	25	7	348	78	365	285	139	301	124	24	154	
Al Ain	182	147	330	232	256	176	221	256	195	131		
Dubai	49	17	324	102	264	184	154	264	127			
Fujairah	119	110	491	115	484	404	26	391				
Hameem	313	281	276	366	62	142	418					
Khor Fakkan	146	137	518	148	511	431						
Madinat Zayid	233	201	136	286	80							
Mezaira'a	377	345	212	430								
Ra's al-Khaimah	62	85	426									
Ruwais	373	341										
Sharjah	32											

About the author

Gareth Leggett was literally born on the move. He was only two weeks old when his mother returned to Jeddah, Saudi Arabia from a short-pit stop to give birth in London. Throughout his childhood he and his family wandered the globe. From six to nine he explored the Highlands of Papua New Guinea, while his pre-teen years were spent in the deserts of Sudan and the lowlands of Scotland. As a teenager, he lived in Singapore and here his life-long love affair with windsurfing began. Thus, he took numerous trips to Malaysia in the search of the elusive perfect combination of wind and wave.

Back in Scotland to complete his education, Gareth vowed to choose a career that would permit him to continue travelling and, after completing his hospitality management diploma, he followed his parents to Australia in search of new open spaces and especially open water. Even within Australia, however, the Leggett wanderlust was unquenched and the family 'legged' it from Sydney to Rockhampton Queensland (where Gareth obtained his IT degree) and finally to Adelaide. Australia's wide open-spaces did not daunt Gareth as he revelled in driving for hours, even completing the drive from Rockhampton to Adelaide (some 3000 kms) stopping only for petrol over 30 hours. Reader beware, this should not be attempted by the normal! If you were to put a pin in the middle of Australia that would probably be where Gareth had yet another adventure losing two tyres off the rim driving from Uluru (Ayers Rock) to Alice Springs. As he had only one spare tyre, he had to wait four hours in the desert for a passer-by to find help.

But even the vastness of Australia was not enough for this intrepid explorer. Africa beckoned and Gareth travelled to South Africa, where he worked as a software tester and met his second great love, me! Gareth's patience and thoroughness became evident, not only in his doggedness in finding every bug in the computer programmes and systems he tested, but also in his tenacity in tracking down and shooting (with a camera of course) wildlife in South Africa. Having driven round exploring every highway and byway of South Africa for two years, next he was sent to Holland, while I went to work as an English lecturer in Oman.

Finally, we met up again and married in Australia before I awoke his wanderlust again with my tales of Arabia. In Al Ain, as a trailing spouse, Gareth was confronted with a sea of dunes, rather than waves and with no software to test, he started testing the vast and untapped road network of the UAE. Here he found fascinating spots all on tarmac, which many people still believe are inaccessible except by 4-wheel drive. The fact that I am a severely directionally challenged navigator 'tested' this tester, so he decided to create **On-Road in the UAE**, a guide to provide simple, user-friendly step-by-step directions to some of these interesting locations.

Michelle Picard
Al Ain 2005

Contact Gareth at onroadintheuae@hotmail.com

Notes

Notes